Marketing Advice For Independent Restaurants That Has *Proven Successful* in the Real World... Not Just *Tested* In A College Classroom

This book IS about successful, proven, online and offline marketing strategies guaranteed to simply and quickly fill your restaurant fast, without wasting thousands of dollars on radio, TV, and other advertising that doesn't work.

This book IS NOT a marketing advice textbook found in college classrooms that teaches theories that work well on paper, but not in the Real world.

This book IS a Real-World, common sense book which understands that you, the independent restaurant owner, is short on time and resources. This book teaches you Fast, Proven, and Simple marketing strategies that work NOW, bring in loads of new guests nightly, and teaches you how to retain your existing guests. This book teaches you all this quickly, simply and easily... all without breaking the bank.

WHAT YOU WILL LEARN

▸ How to simply and easily bring back your best guests night after night with fun and exciting promotions.

▸ How to use the #1 holiday in the world to attract happy new guests to your restaurant on a daily basis.

▸ How to put your restaurant in front of the 500 million users of Facebook... with no website required!

▸ How to show up near the top of all search engines so more potential local guests can find you online.

FULL

A Complete Online & Offline Roadmap
to Marketing Your Independent
Restaurant

By Dean Killingbeck
And Mark Ijlal

With special contributions from
Urvi Mehta and Jacqueline Shaffer

Authors Online!

For updates and more resources,
Visit our book's website at

TheFullRestaurantBook.com/ActionPlan

ISBN: 978-0-9831585-0-9

Library of Congress Control Number: 201091732

CONTENTS

SECTION 3:

About the Authors

DEAN KILLINGBECK is a business owner and entrepreneur owning and operating four separate businesses. He has personally helped 738 Independent Restaurant Owners discover the simple and easy way to retain existing guests and acquire new ones filling those empty seats all week long and not just on weekends. He also is a noted speaker and has shared the stage with the Zig Zigler, Dan Kennedy, Bill Glazer and other noted marketing guru's.

MARK IJLAL came to America with just $243 and a desire to find a better life for himself. After six years of working minimum wage jobs, he started his first business of buying and selling real estate in Detroit. Within 6 months he quit his job and started his first company. Eight years later, his business adventures include ownership of 5 businesses so far. In his early days, like everybody else, he used to dream about having enough money one day to be able to do radio and TV advertising but then he started teaching himself how to use online marketing strategies to grow his business and his company sales and profits started to grow. He has been blogging for six years now, has over 250 online videos on YouTube and iTunes and speaks frequently at business conferences and seminars about online marketing. Mark lives in Metro Detroit and actively manages his own businesses.

About the Guest Contributors

URVI MEHTA *is a passionate Social Media Evangelist who thrives on teaching and consulting business owners and organizations on how to effectively use Web 2.0, social media marketing tools and social networks like Facebook, Twitter and LinkedIn to create buzz, traffic and profits while increasing their branding online.*

Urvi Mehta is a co-founder of PR Easy. PR Easy is the client focused full service internet marketing company which serves clients in US, Canada, UK and Australia. At PR Easy we provide Training, Consulting and various Done-4-You services which radically increase client's presence online which gets them massive exposure and web traffic to their website. PR Easy focuses on creating marketing campaigns which results into very qualified prospects for their clients thus increasing client's bottom line. PR Easy provides Search Engine Marketing, Search Engine Optimization, Social Media Marketing and Landing Page Creation services to business owners.

Discover How Restaurant owners are using Facebook fan page right now to bring more patrons to their business and create raving fans that come back over and over again.

*Visit http://www.PReasy.com/restaurantmarketing to download A FREE Training Video On **"5 Key Elements Restaurant Owners Should Have On Their Facebook Fan Page"***

JACQUELINE SHAFFER *helps independent restaurant owners get more customers through targeted local search marketing integrated with online and offline marketing strategies.*

With her 'Find Me Famous' services, she helps businesses cultivate a strong local presence – to become Famous - in their

iv

own cities, so they are found first and most often by customers looking for their specialty.

Being found at the top of online searches is just one component of a multi-faceted approach she uses with restaurant owners to reach maximum local exposure that gets more guests seated everyday.

When she's not helping business owners to get locally famous, she's a soccer mom, rollerblading fanatic and enjoys investing in real estate. She currently resides in SE Michigan with her husband, son and retriever, Casey.

Visit www.FindMeFamous.com/Restaurants to learn more about local search marketing services provided by her company.

CHAPTER 1
The #1 Most Celebrated Restaurant Holiday in the World!
by Dean Killingbeck

One of my favorite things to do is ask independent restaurant owners, "What is the most celebrated holiday in the world and how can you cash in on it?" It's a loaded question, because I already know that 96% will get it wrong with answers like Mother's Day, New Years Eve, Easter, and St. Patrick's Day (usually only the bar owners throw that one in). Secondly, I can look like a smarty pants (but since I'm a nice guy, I don't rub it in) when I tell them they are 100% wrong. The right answer is **BIRTHDAYS**!

Birthdays are the most celebrated holidays in the world.

I might be exaggerating a little to call birthdays "holidays," as they might more accurately be considered an "event." But, since I think *my* birthday should be considered a national holiday, I'm sure others think their birthdays are holidays too! The best part is...*everybody* has one! Want even *more* good news? With more than a *cajillion* people in the US ("cajillion" is retired farmer lingo for a whole lot!), a birthday happens every day of the week, every month, all year long! What does that mean to you? As a restaurant owner, you can benefit from the predictive frequency and increased cash flow generated by a birthday program. Also, the ramped up business keeps your staff sharp, keeps their pockets bulging with tips, and keeps them happy so they don't start a mutiny over "petty little things" they would have time to focus on if they weren't busy!

Birthday Programs Are A No Brainer Goldmine.

Anybody who pays attention to what I have to share can turn a nice little birthday system into a goldmine. How? Consider this fact: according to the National Restaurant Association, the average birthday guest celebrates their birthday with 2.8 family and friends, for a total guest count of 3.8. Consequently, that means you have a lot of "four-toppers" coming through your door! Isn't that what you want? Best of all, they're out to celebrate and have a good time (in other words, pinching pennies is not their top priority), so your servers can "up sell" all day long! After all…your birthday guest only has a birthday once a year and they should splurge, right? Having tables with that "splurge" mentality every single night, week after week, makes a birthday program a No Brainer!

One of our typical restaurant responses is:

> *With just ONE MONTH behind us using your promotion, we had 99 customers come in with your certificates! That's a redemption rate of 25% and a boost in sales of around $8,000! The best part of your promotion is these were actually NEW customers, who have never been to our restaurant before! Giving them a gift for their birthday was a great first impression! Thanks for a great marketing idea that really WORKS!*
>
> *Angelo and Renia Marini, Sal E Pepe Restaurant & Bar, Newtown CT*

You Look Like A Super Hero!

What other advantages (besides increased guest count, increased cash flow, and happy staff members) does a birthday program have? Think about this: it's your birthday next week and

I just sent you a birthday gift. Are you happy? Of course you are! How about I send you *money*? Are you doing a happy dance now? Heck yeah, you are (just please close the blinds, the neighbors are watching)!

EVERYONE loves to get presents! When you give someone a birthday present, you've done two things: you made *them* feel special, and made *yourself* look good. Think about it...outside of their family and close friends, who else knew it was their birthday? Probably not a whole lot of people! But you did, *and* you sent them a present. Now, in their eyes, getting a Free Dinner on their birthday is found money! However, in your eyes, you know your food costs aren't nearly as much as you charge for your entrées, which should run around +/- 30%, but the perceived value of your gift is enormous! And, with the "celebrators" that the birthday person brings along with them, you're coming out the winner tenfold, because the celebrators are paying full price! Add to that, everyone is thankful that you thought of them on their birthday...and you are creating **relationships**, one of the most important building blocks of your business.

NOTE: Don't strive for the one-time sale; strive for the lifetime guest – the one who will visit your restaurant for years to come.

The Ol' Glory Days Are Behind Us

It used to be that a decent location, good food, and a friendly staff were all that was needed to have a successful restaurant. Nowadays, with the big chain restaurants and their trillion-dollar advertising budgets overwhelming your potential guests with non-stop "food porn" and discounted deals on the TV, radio, and newspaper, you must focus on relationship building. A Birthday Program helps you do just that. When done right, a local independent restaurant (even in a small community) can expect to have 80 to 120 new guests walking through their front door every month! Do the math: that's about one thousand per year! What's even better is the nature of this holiday – every day, month after month of every year, somebody is celebrating a birthday.

The Making of a Great Birthday Program

You're probably wondering why everyone isn't using birthday programs all over the country. What we've found is that most restaurant owners know about birthday promotions and some have even tried them. The problem is they've either run into a variety of roadblocks or have trouble getting a system or set of procedures in place to implement the program. So here's what I'm going to do for you...I'm going to spell out **exactly** what you need and don't need to make birthdays one of your best "cash cow" moneymakers.

✓ Get the right list (who's the best customer)

✓ Give the guest an irresistible offer (get them off the couch and away from the Wii)

✓ Develop the letter with a gift certificate inviting the guest into your restaurant

Let's consider some of the tactics for using a good, rock-solid birthday promotion for getting **new** guests. Later in the book, I'll discuss using birthdays for your current "house list" and loyal patrons, but for right now, let's focus on New Guest Acquisition; getting those first timers (and a bunch of their friends) ready to have a good time and spend lots of money.

4

Obtaining The List

The Most Important aspect of the birthday program (and ANY program) is defining your very best guest. Let me explain what I mean by "best guest" because it will be different for different types of restaurants in different areas. This is definitely not a "one size fits all." Besides, that's not how real marketing works anyway. Okay, so what do I mean? All restaurants have a specific guest *demographic*. Some people say I obsess on the subject of demographics and list selection (in fact, I sometimes dream about demographics, which upsets my wife, but that's a different book).

NOTE: If you want a good campaign, you better have a great list.

With any type of marketing, when it comes to obtaining a list, you're better off targeting a narrow niche (aka "rifle approach") than you are mailing to "just anybody" (aka "the shotgun approach"). The shotgun approach scatters your message out there to everyone, including the "coupon-clippers" (who only eat out when there is a coupon), the "gray hairs" (who split their meals and never eat after 4pm), the "young guns" (the 18 to 20-somethings that are so broke they can't even afford peanut butter on a regular basis), and other undesirables (we call them "bottom feeders," lovingly, of course). Your offer was *amazing* for them, but lousy for you because you just paid for that guest who's not going to come back until the next special offer (and who needs that?). What you should be looking for, with any marketing campaign, is to target the guest that best fits your demographics, and then, of course, turn them into a loyal, repeat guest.

But Everyone Eats At My Restaurant!

You may be thinking, "But Dean, I get *everybody* in my restaurant from 8 to 80 years of age!" Well, you could be right, but if you're going to spend your hard-earned money on marketing, you need to get the best results, so let's change your thinking. When you think of all the guests who come into your restaurant, think of a bell curve (or the shape of my stomach after a great meal). A long time ago you probably learned about the 20/80 rule – or the 80/20 rule if you went to school in Detroit (that's my hometown, so don't send me any nasty emails saying I'm mad at Detroit).

Either way you learned it – 20/80 or 80/20 – it's basically the same concept: 80% of your business is done by 20% of your people. Another way to say it... 20% of your guests makes up 80% of your profit. Sure, you have guests from all over the spectrum of the demographic pipeline, but if you're talking dollars taken in, you're best served focusing on the top 20%, not the marginal 80%. When you're thinking of this elite 20%, consider the top three demographics:

1. Are they Homeowners? Homeowners (people who own a house or condo) are more likely to stay in your area and remain a loyal guest than someone who is an apartment renter.

2. What is their approximate household income? Try to figure out this number without demanding they hand over their 1040 tax forms (you may get thrown in the clink!).

3. What is the age range? Is it 18 to 30-somethings? 30-55? People tend to have different dining habits depending on their age.

For unique establishments, these principles can be skewed somewhat, but these are the basic facts you can effectively start with. Base your restaurant demographics on the top 20% of your bell curve to match your ideal guest. Forget about the other 80%... cut them out of your budget of time, money, and effort, and allow yourself to focus on turning your business into an extraordinary money-making machine. Obviously, most restaurant owners don't use the 80/20 rule in their marketing. That's why some restaurant owners struggle just to survive, working harder, not working smarter.

Family Dining vs. High-End Demographics

As an example, let's take two restaurants to compare and contrast; one is a family-style restaurant, and the other a high-end restaurant. The family restaurant's ideal guest comes from a household made up of married adults, earning more than $45,000 a year, between the ages of 35 and 55, who own their home and have children. Now, the high-end restaurant (by high-end, let's say an entrée starts at $22 and goes all the way up to $55-$60) has a demographic that is radically different from the family style restaurant. In making a list selection for our "high end" restaurant example, we will look for a slightly older age selection with more discretionary income. We'll probably first look at the 45-65 year old who owns their own home and has a household income of $100,000 or more. It's true that the same households could appear on both lists, and that's okay. As long as the demographics match up, both restaurants can have a phenomenally successful program.

Where They Live Does Make A Difference!

One last thing regarding demographics: to start, stick to the 1 to 5 mile radius rule of thumb. Naturally, all restaurants have the "exception-to-the-rule guest" coming from much further away and that's fine. However, to maximize your return-on-investment (ROI), you must first focus your efforts on what empirical evidence has proven to generate the highest rate of return. For me or anybody else to suggest differently would make us hacks, quacks, or wannabe marketers, and not a pro. Also, speaking of hacks, quacks, and wannabes…be sure you purchase your list from a reputable broker. The difference in list quality varies with each company, so do some homework and spend your money wisely.

5 Secret Strategies to Creating the All-Important Mailer

When creating the All-Important Mailer, my clients prefer to send a full-color letter and gift certificate in a business-size #10 envelope. This lets them not only personalize the envelope (to make it seem handwritten and ensure it gets opened), but the letter gives them the room to tell their story, enticing the guest to come and see what they are all about, and tells the guest – making it believable – why they are receiving a birthday offer. A great handbook on how to create an effective letter is Dan Kennedy's book, *The Ultimate Sales Letter*.

Secret Strategy #1: Personalization

In a world where the word "secret" is overused, I do have a real "secret" the vast majority of business owners don't understand. Your mailers **must be** customized and personalized to the intended recipient, which includes the outside of the envelope, the letter inside, and the certificate.

BONUS STRATEGY

You are trying to initiate a relationship between the birthday guest and yourself. You are **personally** introducing **your** local restaurant, which psychologically encourages them to "participate in the community" by visiting you instead of a big chain restaurant. With all the distrust throughout the country for greedy Big Businesses, you don't want to look like a "chain."

Do you think the big chain restaurants tell the birthday guest who the manager is at their local store when they send an offer? NOPE! Because nine out of ten times it doesn't come from the local chain; it's being mass-mailed from some corporate office a *cajillion* miles away where they send one generic mailer addressed to "Dear Occupant." As much as I HATE that greeting, "Dear Occupant," you can bet I LOVE when the chains use it. It makes the independent businesses look that much better when they personalize their mailers. Remember, you are striving for a long-term relationship.

Why is personalization so important? According to Direct Marketing Magazine, response rates jump 30% just by using this personalization strategy. It will cost more in time and effort, but consider the numbers. Don't forget you're using the rifle approach, not the shotgun approach.

An example of the shotgun approach: take 10,000 cheap little 3x5 postcards that cost a nickel to print, the 28-cent postcard stamp, costing you a total of $3,300 for the mailing in the hopes of getting a miniscule response. These postcards aren't going to the guests that you hand-picked, ensuring a great future guest; these are sent generically to everyone. That's a great way to be "penny wise and pound foolish" and more than likely lose a lot of money with false economics. I would much rather see someone invest in the right list, create the letter and offer correctly, mail 300 of them a month, and get a consistent 20% response.

Granted, the personalized mailers will cost $1.50 or more each to get everything right (the right list, using personalization, printing with handwritten fonts, stuffing and stamping with over-sized postal stamps); however, the initial investment is much lower than the cheap postcards, and the immediate return is incredible. Also, it can be repeated monthly (anyone can duplicate the system), and the lifetime value of the guests the program brings in is worth several times more than any other marketing.

Secret Strategy #2: "The Look"

As mentioned earlier, the piece you mail shouldn't look "corporate" or "slick." Strive for the look and feel of a mailer that came right out of your back office. You *must* use "real" stamps, preferably an oversized commemorative stamp, put on crooked, so it looks like you put it on by hand (not by machine).

Never, EVER use a postal meter, internet stamps, the cheesy flag stamp (that looks just like a bulk mail stamp) or bulk indicia. Also, use hand-written fonts to personalize your envelope, not some cheap typewriter font. Now, if you think these little details are unnecessary and expensive time wasters…you're wrong. Empirical evidence has proven that these theories get your mail OPENED, and no amount of excuses, laziness, or cost cutting tactics will make up for the lost ROI from not ensuring this is done right. The sooner a restaurant learns these methods, the sooner they will start making *real* money. I understand that for many people this is counterintuitive, but it works! Also, don't be surprised when you get feedback from your family or business associates that you are a little "off" for doing your marketing this way. Unfortunately, a real "herd mentality" exists and people feel safer and more secure doing what has always been done before. The proof is really in the "pudding," and when the resulting increased sales start happening with greater and greater frequency, you will never go back to the old ways of marketing. In fact, feel free to do the "Na-na-na-na-naaaa-na!" I-Told-You-So dance.

Secret Strategy #3: The Irresistible Offer.

It's all in the Psychology. Why do guests respond so well to Birthday Programs, generating a minimum 10% to as high as 37% redemption rates? Because, guaranteed, no one else invites them to come into their restaurant on their birthday. Okay…if you happen to be a Bed, Bath, and Beyond™ customer, then you get a 20% coupon to use in the store. But does that make you feel special? No! Because EVERYONE gets the same 20% coupons four times a year in the mail whether they're a customer or not!

A common mistake I see is restaurant owners not giving the new guest a completely "Outrageous" offer to come and dine at their restaurant for the first time. Remember, the public is extremely skeptical and they're also easily bored of seeing the same offers over and over again: "buy one get one free" (in their eyes that means they'll get sucked into spending a lot of money because your restaurant must be SO expensive); "half off" (why bother?), and more ("Receive a FREE sample of shoe polish, just for stopping by!"). They get so fatigued from seeing the same old lame offers, weasel clauses, and fine print that contains a ton of disclaimers, that they start ignoring all offers.

Make Them Feel Special!

BONUS STRATEGY

After your birthday guest finishes their dinner, give everyone in the party a Thank You Bounce Back Coupon to receive ½ off an entrée on their next visit (of course, they have to come back within the next two weeks, and only one coupon per family). The experts say that if you can get a guest to come back to your restaurant more than three times in a short period, they will have formed a habit, and are well on their way to become a loyal, lifetime guest. And, isn't that why you spend money on marketing? To get Loyal, Lifetime Guests?

The goal isn't to acquire guests that only come in when you're having a special. Remember, guests are fickle...they will take the easiest route, most times relying on their kids to tell them where to go for dinner (more than likely to avoid the battle).

Additional Bonus Strategy: Develop a Kid's Club because kids are a vital part of the new economy!

Here's the big AH-HA! Make the birthday person feel special and give them an irresistible offer that gets them off the couch, away from the Wii, into the car, and into your restaurant! You have to motivate their butts to move. Heck, we already know that 2.8 people come in with the birthday person, and like I asked before... who doesn't want a herd of four-toppers strolling in ready to spend money? So, what are you willing to do to get those four-toppers in your restaurant?

Give them a **Free Entrée** and be sure the dollar value of your free entrée allows them to order from at least 80% of your menu items (if your mouth just dropped open, feel free to push it closed and keep reading). Why such a high offer? The worst thing you can do with a birthday program is invite a guest to come and get a free entrée for their birthday and when they get there, the only thing that is actually free is a small side salad or a small pasta dish. If you're in the business of making people angry, that's the way to do it, but it's not the way to gain future loyal, money-making guests. It doesn't matter if you're a family-style, high-end, or counter-served restaurant…this principal works for everyone. Psychologically, you must not be cheap with your birthday offer. Remember, you want them to come back again and again.

Secret Strategy #4: No Weasel Clauses!

Nothing punches someone in the gut more than when they read they've been offered something spectacular, and then continue on reading to find exemptions and strings that are attached (i.e., only available between the hours of 3:15 and 3:30, Mondays and Wednesdays). Basically, anything tied to or obligating them to make additional purchases will suppress your results.

So as to be sparkling clear, let me say it again – "**No Strings Attached!**" You need to get them excited! New guest acquisition is not the time to be cheap. Understand that you are "buying their business," so get over yourself. Remember; if you bring in the right person, their lifetime value is staggering. ,So, how much are you willing to spend to get a lifetime guest? You must be willing to spend five, seven, or even ten dollars to get that loyal customer in your door the first time, but the smart business person understands that you are making a sale to gain a lifetime guest… NOT getting a guest to make a one-time sale.

Secret Strategy #5: Post it on the Fridge!

When creating your mailer, include a gift certificate with your offer whenever possible. Why? So your guest can discard your letter after they've read it, and post the certificate on their refrigerator. That's where all the important stuff goes: kid's drawings, pictures of grandkids, doctor appointment reminders, and all the other important things (like checks from the government...HAHAHA! That was a knee-slapper!). If you include your offer in a letter, the chances are huge that the letter will be shoved into a drawer (because it's too bulky to stick on the fridge). However, a 4x8½ cardstock certificate will lay nice and not take up valuable fridge space, yet still be visible as a reminder to your guest every single day until they use their birthday certificate.

Make It Happen!

In closing, it's a shame so many restaurants don't understand how to market a birthday program correctly, or take the step and hire a competent company to do it for them. A lot of money and entire restaurants are lost because of it. That being said, it's important for you to know it's not your fault, up until this point. (After this point, it's all your fault! Just kidding.)

Restaurant owners, for the most part, have never been trained to be marketers. It isn't taught in culinary art schools, colleges, or even business schools (unless you go to school for restaurant-specific marketing). Basic marketing and advertising might be given a little attention, but the material is so generic, it might as well be useless. Worse yet, examples and models that *are* given, are textbook examples of huge corporations that have multi-million dollar ad budgets, many locations to divide up costs, better media buying power, and a vested interest to do brand building. Like I said before, past generations of fathers, great grandfathers, and distant relatives only needed a decent location, good food, and a friendly staff. Well, we're in the 21st century and the rules have changed!

As an independent restaurant owner, you can effectively compete, but you must use different strategies. Call your strategies "No Holds Barred," "stealth," "guerrilla," heck, go dress like a ninja…whatever you want. My point is, move faster, use a highly-targeted approach, and do *everything* you can to maximize your ROI.

In a later chapter, I'll explain how *not* to be an advertising victim, subject to the whim of any and all media reps that show up at your front door. Be strong, grasshopper.

NOTE: One of the biggest mistakes independent restaurant owners make is not following the correct recipe.

Let's face it – everyone has an opinion and thinks they are a marketing "expert." By nature as business owners, we tend to be a little stubborn and that's not a bad thing. However, much like a recipe to bake bread, if you put the yeast in cold water and not hot, the bread will not rise. Similarly with marketing, there is a definite "right way" and many "wrong ways." Following the right procedures, in the correct order at the right time is what makes it work. It's not difficult…all it takes is a little discipline to "git-er-done" (like one of those redneck guys likes to say).

Using the right recipe, a new customer birthday mailer can work like a charm, or it can flop if some knucklehead screws up the recipe and starts using postal indicias, metered mail, mass mail labels; or doesn't personalize the offers, using words like "Dear Occupant." Aghhh. Any or all of these otherwise good intentioned excuses for laziness will cause a program to flop. I guess that's why every restaurant in American doesn't do a birthday program... because they can't follow the recipe. That's okay by me and should be for you too. Decide to be in the top 3% of income earners by following these procedures and enjoy the learning process; you will be well paid for it.

My company gets success stories all the time from our clients and I'm always glad to hear from them. We have clients who are able to increase their business by 40% with better margins, are able to earn twice as much as previous years, and become debt free just by using our birthday program for new guest acquisition. One member stands out in my mind as somebody whose restaurant was brought back from the brink of disaster.

Jeff Hersha of Bradley, Illinois (a northwest suburb of Chicago) owns a Mancino's restaurant, serving pizzas and grinder sub sandwiches for a sit-down or carry-out family friendly market. Jeff had a great location...he was in a strip mall, with the local Walmart as the anchor store, which attracted thousands of people everyday past his location. Needless to say, he had a very good business. Then one day he got some very bad news. Walmart decided to move two miles down the road and become a Super WalMart. When that happened, his business plummeted by a blood chilling 70%! He was stuck in a strip mall with an empty WalMart store, and his lease and build out expenses did not make moving to another location a viable option. Now, Jeff was already aware of new guest acquisition and the principles of a good birthday program, but the Walmart catastrophe served as a great motivator to get him moving with his marketing. I'm happy to share that within a very short time frame, Jeff was able to get his gross sales and profit back up to the pre-Walmart exodus, in the same location! His business is growing with a better, more loyal, high

16

paying clientele than before, and he has a much greater sense of confidence in himself and his business and in how he can comfortably provide for his family in the coming years.

Zig Zigler says, *"It's better to dig your well before you're thirsty."* You can bet that there are many people right now in your community just waiting to celebrate their birthdays today; there will be just as many tomorrow, and the day after. So what are you waiting for?

ACTION PLAN

1. Who's your best guest?

    Demographics: age_____

    Income _____

    Radius from restaurant _____

    Homeowner? _____

    Children present _____

2.   Find a List Broker to help you with your selection.

3.   Develop a mailer with an irresistible offer.

4.   Implement the program (mail the dang thing!!!)

Want more information? FREE samples of mailers? Go to
TheFullRestaurantBook.com/ActionPlan

CHAPTER 2
The #2 Best New Guest Acquisition System
by Dean Killingbeck

There's nothing wrong with getting up early and working hard, just don't forget to use your God-given brain for what it was intended for... thinking. – Dean Killingbeck

In the first chapter we talked about using birthdays as the #1 best new guest acquisition system. I hope you retained that valuable information and learned some new techniques on how to implement your own successful birthday program...in fact, what are you doing still reading? You should be working on your birthday program! Jeesh! Well, I guess I can cut you a break this time...more than likely it's after 10pm, you're waiting for your waitstaff to finish cleaning up, and you have a spare 10 minutes to read...and what else should you be reading other than this fantastic book, right? Besides, you're so smart, you've already started working on your own birthday program and are well on your way to success. Well, in this chapter, we'll discuss how to acquire MORE new guests by using the #2 best system: New Homeowners.

But Dean, why do I need MORE new guests?

WOW! What a great question (see how smart you are?). To answer that, let me share with you a sobering statistic:

YOU ARE THEORETICALLY LOSING 49% OF YOUR REGULAR GUESTS EACH YEAR.

I know that was a bit dramatic, but it's true... here's how it stacks up:

✓ The United States Postal Service tells us that 12 to 22% of the population decides to move every year. I bet they didn't even consult with you to see if that would hurt your business, did they? Don't worry, they didn't ask me either!

✓ Because of family circumstances (kids going off to college, divorce, job loss, retirement, etc.), another 15% are **forced** to change their lifestyles and may not be able to eat out as often. Lord knows this is happening across the country at an alarming rate. Think a "restaurant bailout" is on the way? HA! Think again!

✓ Others just forget about you; either they got tired of coming to the same old place, or you didn't make them feel special; this accounts for an additional 10% loss. Shame on you! (I'm saying that with my "Big Loud Voice.")

✓ Worst of all, those big chain restaurants are continually trying to steal your best guests away...and they're successful! With their huge, million dollar marketing budgets, they are able to buy endless TV ads, full color glossy ads that are stuck in every newspaper, and more. Those dirty little tricks lead to losing a whopping 10% annually. That one hurts, doesn't it?

So, now that you're aware HOW you're losing loads of guests every year, can you now see why you need more than one system in place to counteract the total guest losses and get an abundant amount of new guests to fill their spots? Of course you do, because you're a smart business owner. The old story goes: the restaurant owner and the marketing consultant were talking...the restaurant owner asks the consultant, "What is your best way to get 100 new guests?" The consultant responds, "I don't have one way to get you 100 new guests, but I have 100 ways to get one new guest!" The moral of the story is: You Need More Than One System In Place!

A new homeowner system is another strategy in new guest acquisition. What makes it so special? New homeowner guests are ten times more loyal.. Also, they aren't loyal to a restaurant yet, so the competition is thin. New people move into your area every day of every month, as predictably as the sun rises and sets each day. This "mover" market represents one of the greatest opportunities to capture the ideal guest at the perfect time; when they are establishing their habits and deciding their favorite places to go for their meals. However, your timing has to be right...sort of like fishing: even with the best bait, if the water is too hot or too cold, the fish won't bite. Well, the same concept goes for the new homeowner guest...hit them too early and they're too busy to think about you. Hit them too late, and they may already have a favorite restaurant.

Today in our new and emerging economy, there is a "right way" and a "wrong way" to utilize this mover market as an independent restaurant owner. The "wrong way" will keep you frustrated and convinced that "marketing" doesn't work for you. The "right way" will make you a ton of money and keep you smiling and confident. I'll show you the right way to use a *new homeowner program*.

One of the most valuable pieces of advice I share with restaurant owners is that I actually correct some of the inaccurate thinking they are taught about new homeowner marketing. Many marketers and list brokers, motivated by the quantity of what they are selling and not the quality, will sell you a "new mover list or program," but you should actually be interested in "new *homeowners marketing.*" There is a distinct difference between new movers and *new homeowners*, and how you make your list selection is crucial. Not all "movers" are created equal. While discussing your list and demographics, just like with a successful birthday program, there are four vital selects to consider: 1) proximity; 2) income; 3) age; and 4) if they own their own home. These 'selects' make up the four legs of a chair...take one leg away and the chair falls over.

As you've read previously, the select I put as highest priority over income and age, is that the person must own their own home. Here's why: if you mass market all "new movers," you include everybody that moves into your community, with no regard to whether they moved into an apartment, trailer, student housing, or rented a room in a red light district (just kidding...I was just making sure you're still paying attention). There are numerous people you shouldn't waste your time, money, and effort marketing to. Now, I'm not making a value or moral judgment (again, please don't send any angry emails or hate mail), and you may not mind them coming into your restaurant to spend their money. However, let me share with you some statistics to support my stance on home ownership: as a general rule, people who own their own home behave differently than renters.

Looking at the statistics purely from the best sources of information (which are actual results, not the statistics from some math geek from Harvard), we have an exceptional deliverability rate with homeowners. Our list broker actually guarantees 97% delivery to homeowners, which gives us 97% of our mail being delivered, leaving only 3% as undeliverable. All reputable list brokers update their mover data monthly and are highly accurate, leaving "homeowner" undeliverables less than 3%, and never more than a still acceptable 5%. With the various "all new movers" lists (that include renters), it is not uncommon to have a 10-20% undeliverable rate. No list broker will ever tell you that little truth, but I've fielded enough phone calls from other people's customers complaining about "actual deliverability" rates of renters from other brokers who don't segment their list.

Combine that with the fact that many apartment complexes have an excess of 20% vacancy rates. The chances that your mail could be forwarded to somebody that has possibly moved hundreds of miles away, or who doesn't fit your age and income demographics, is highly likely. That high undeliverable rate means one important thing: wasted money on mailers that don't get delivered. Also, people who own their own home or condominium tend to become much more established in a community and on average, stay in that home 5 years longer than a renter. They also tend to have greater influence over the purchase decisions of others, meaning more referral guests for you...which equals more four toppers!

You also must consider the lifetime value (LTV) of your guest. An average renter stays put for only 12-18 months, while an average homeowner stays five to seven years. Doesn't it make sense to spend your hard-earned money on a guest that will be around for a few years, instead of a few months? Learn more about the LTV of your guest in Appendix A in the back of the book.

All those factors directly affect your ROI from your direct mail offers and believe me, with renters, it's tough to make any real money with those odds stacked against you. So, understand that I'm not being judgmental or biased. However, as a smart, savvy and accurate thinking entrepreneur, you need to look at the "big

22

picture" and what is going to net you the highest payoff and best ROI. So I recommend to you, and whoever else is reading this book with you, to only market to **new homeowners**. Skip the renters.

Fortunately, through years of testing (and back-breaking hard work, pain, suffering, and did I mention back-breaking hard work?) hundreds of thousands of pieces mailed for hundreds of our successful clients, we have "cracked the code" on how to make this a surefire, guaranteed system. Executing the system correctly will mean every month new "ideal guests" will walk into your business ready, willing, and able to be on your growing list of "best guest regulars." In this chapter, I am going to tell you exactly how we do it, so you can do it too!

> *I wanted to let you know about our Birthday and New Homeowner campaigns. Both of them have been a great success with the birthday mailers receiving approximately 15% to 16% redemption rates and new homeowner mailers just slightly lower. We are very pleased with the results. Both systems make us money and continue to bring in a boat-load of new guests, which is exactly what we need!*

> *Also, our new guests have been complimenting us on the personalization of our mailings. Can you believe they actually noticed all the hard work that you're doing to insure that they open our mailers? Well, keep it up...it's working!*

> *Michael Clark, Ed & Joe's Restaurant, Tinley Park, IL*

The Nitty Gritty – The Nuts and Bolts of the System

Okay, before we get down to the nuts and bolts (crackers and cheese for the restaurateur), keep in mind that I'm teaching you a **system**. Like a cooking recipe, you are given a list of ingredients, utensils needed, as well as an order and process that anybody can follow to achieve predictable results. However, even using the finest ingredients, most expensive utensils, and yes, even the best chef...if any step is altered, reversed, hastened, or skipped, the whole thing can turn into a disaster. With "new homeowners" there is a recipe describing exactly **who, when, what** and **why,** that when followed in the correct sequence, produces the desired results: new, happy homeowners streaming into your restaurant ready to be fed, pampered, and impressed. To be successful...You Must Follow The System!

All right, we have already discussed **"who"** we are targeting. Specifically, for this chapter, that is new homeowners who: a) live within a 1-5 mile radius of your restaurant(s); b) own their own home; c) have the right income to demographically match your type of establishment; and, d) fall within the best age range to match your demographics. We've covered how important your list selection is back in Chapter 1, and I can't stress it enough AGAIN in this chapter.

Now it's time to dig into the **"when."** To better understand the "when" is to better understand the typical process a family goes through when moving to a new home. The fact is, new homeowners initially spend a lot of money on home furnishings, home improvement projects, and appliances during the first few months. As they begin to acclimate to their new surroundings, they're also bombarded with "sales pitches" and offers from a wide variety of businesses with "welcome wagon" type offers. The sheer volume of "stuff" being sent to them on a daily basis is overwhelming, making it difficult to distinguish anything or anyone from the pack (remember, they are being offered everything by everyone). Also, don't forget...most of these households are super busy, having both parents working full-time jobs, raising kids, changing schools, and trying to make their new homes livable.

Through careful testing, we have learned that it's better to start a new mover system in the third month after the guest has moved into their new home. For many ambitious people, that may seem like waiting too long, but trust me, it's not. It's taken us several years of trial and error and comparing notes with a wide variety of service providers to learn the best practices of timing and sequence. It's in the third month that new homeowners really start to feel "settled" and begin getting active in their community. Anytime before that, you end up competing against retailers selling hardware, supplies, drapes and carpeting, which are all that is on a new homeowner's mind. With few exceptions of quick, carry-out and fast food, your best potential guests will not start looking for, or establishing, their long-term places of doing business until they have been in their new home for about three months.

The biggest reason most other new mover programs fail is the way they are executed. Typically the scenario goes something like this:

> An independent restaurant owner receives a call from a sales rep with an "offer" to join a co-op program that has dozens of other local businesses. Restaurateurs are "sold" by ad reps that "...for pennies a household, you get your message delivered." The marketing pieces for all businesses are mailed out and delivered at the same time, in the same small envelope. More times than not, the piece screams "junk mail," and is comprised of the

worst "dear neighbor" offers (scarier yet..."Dear Occupant"). Do the math; those pennies add up to hundreds of dollars that rarely bring in enough business to pay for themselves, let alone make a profit.

The other problem with co-op forms of mass marketing is there's a tendency for guests to rifle through them quickly (usually over the ol' garbage can), selecting only the coupons for businesses they already frequent. They then use those discounts for products and services they planned on paying regular price for, and then chuck the rest of the "coupons" into the trash.

The "lucky" retailer whose coupon gets redeemed ends up losing two ways: first by paying for the ad; and second, by giving a discount to someone who may already be a regular. Not smart advertising.

This is just one of the several ways restaurant owners become "advertising victims." Do not fall victim to these false methods of marketing that only suck your pockets dry and produce little or no results with undesirable guests eating away your profits. Read more about how NOT to become an advertising victim in Chapter 7.

Another problem with mass advertising is that it's usually a one-time mass mailing. As with any marketing, if it's worth doing once, it is usually worth doing a minimum of three times.

To get new homeowners to quit painting the walls and hanging drapes, you must use what we call in the direct mail business, sequential mailers. If you have gone to the expense of buying a list and developing a letter or postcard (by the way, I recommend a letter first), why would you give up after just one mailer?

One thing you need to understand (which I'm sure you're already aware of), is the public as a whole is skeptical and hesitant to believe anything the first time they hear or see it. Consider the upheaval with the banks on Wall Street, dirty politicians, and heck, a famous golfer. Everything seems peachy, then the "Fit hits the Shan," as Toby Keith says. As a result, we, as a community, have become distrustful and shy away from things that are just too good to be true. These folks are busy and you must keep reminding them about your fabulous restaurant!

Three weeks after your initial mailing, remove the names of the guests that responded and mail a second mailer to the rest of the list. In the second mailer, you tell them you "understand" they're busy, but you wanted to give them a second chance to come to your restaurant (because you're just that nice!). Then, three weeks after that, remove the names of the guests that responded to the second mailer and mail a last chance postcard to the rest of the list. You will find that this significantly increases your ROI, plus it lets the new homeowner know you really want their business. It makes them feel special (because you didn't give up on them) and helps to create the relationship that will last a lifetime. With the right system in place, this sequential mailer is executed flawlessly.

Okay, wipe your brow...we've tackled almost all of the steps in our recipe to a Great New Homeowner System. Let's review what we have so far:

> **"Why"** – new homeowners, in essence, are a better overall lifetime guest, spending more money with you than any of your other guests; they help replace all the lost guests you experience throughout the year, and they aren't loyal to another restaurant.

> **"Who"** – only target *homeowners* instead of renters and be sure to select the demographics that best match your favorite guest.

> **"When"** – start your sequence of mailers in the 3rd month after the mover has come into the area.

Which now brings us to the final step..."**What.**" Again, I'll use my "Big Father Voice" and restate loudly that "You Must Have A System." A system by definition is not a one-time event, it's a process of events that leads to desired results. With our new homeowners system, it's not unusual to get a 7-10% response rate on the first mailer, which is a huge statistical victory for anybody in the direct response marketing business, and a great moneymaker for the restaurateur. However, the *real* secret is in the "what" you are sending them. Refer to Chapter 1, and The 5 Secret Strategies to Creating the All Important Mailer. Use those strategies to create your sequential mailers and you are on your way to a successful New Homeowner System!

Don't forget to capture their interest by using the strategies described above and in Chapter 1, to get them to **open** the personalized mail at the right place and right time in their lives (three months after they moved in, use sneak-up mail with real stamps, absolutely NO bulk mail). Also, once the piece is opened (which is half the battle), that's the time to make your outrageous offer and keep them reading…to rope in a lifetime guest… someone who will fall in love with your restaurant and spend a lot of their hard-earned money with you. Remember, your offer should be something so incredible and flattering that they feel magnetically attracted to your place of business. You want them to react like "Wow! This is one nice guy/gal/joint!" You need to get them off their butts, off the couch and, skip the McDonalds™ and Wendys™… and give them something that they'll look forward to doing.

I can't restate enough that you need to be outrageous with your offer(s)…break basically every rule you see other retailers or restaurants doing. Don't use "buy one, get one free" or worse yet, a free appetizer or soft drink. B-O-R-I-N-G and C-H-E-A-P! Offers are all about feelings and you want them to feel like you are a nice guy, not a cheapskate! I recommend offers for free entrées. Yes, a totally free entrée…no weasel clauses, or exemptions. So, as an example, my really outrageous offer would be:

"Come on in and enjoy anything on our menu as our gift to you…FREE, with no strings attached, as our way of welcoming you to the area. No need to buy anything else…just come enjoy yourself and become one of the family!"

Now, that means if most every meal on your menu is priced at twenty or twenty-five dollars, you give it to them! Be sure that your offer allows the guest to choose from approximately 80% of your menu. Remember, impress that new homeowner and they'll share the experience with their circle of influence.

Okay, There Is One "Exemption." The only "exemption" that you must stick to with your offer is a **deadline**. Keep the offer valid for 2 to 4 weeks, creating a reasonable sense of urgency on their part. If you extend your offer for any longer than 4 weeks, chances are the guest will forget about it…the certificate looks so "natural" there on the fridge that it becomes part of the fridge and the guest doesn't notice it anymore.

Be In It For The Long Haul. Unfortunately, with this system, one of the things I sometimes hear is "I think I'm losing money!" But, that's not accurate thinking. Again, almost everyone brings someone with them when they redeem their certificate, meaning you have one guest receiving a FREE entrée and one paying full price, so basically you're breaking even. Also, you need to remember that you received that other full paying guest for FREE because they tagged along with your new homeowner! This outrageous offer is going in the mail only to your ideal, demographically-matched guest; with the proximity, homeownership, income, and age all matched up perfectly to your best regular guest. Most of these ideal new homeowners will have a spouse, significant other, children, or new friends that will eat with them because, realistically, it's rare that any of these guests will dine by themselves. If the average group is a table of three or four, you're "giving" one entrée away, while the table is purchasing 2 to 3 other entrées at full price, along with drinks and/or appetizers. This makes your discount better than any "typical" two-for-one offer or 20% discount. It's a win/win…they feel great, you become the hero, and they'll tell everybody they know about the great meal and experience they had at your restaurant. The economics work out to your advantage. Add in the follow-up marketing you can do, and the various "bounce back" programs you can utilize, and by the time they've eaten at your restaurant three times, you should have a "regular" loyal guest worth thousands.

Wrapping It Up

So, that's what you should be looking for when doing a new homeowner program. You're looking to give them a WOW experience, so they come back again and again, becoming loyal guests, and increasing your bottom line. Be the hero in your neighborhood by welcoming them to your community. Make them feel warm and welcome by "breaking bread" in your establishment. Give them an outrageous offer to "win" them over as a person that delivers on their promises and you'll be well on your way to having a loyal guest for life. Do not give them any reason to be skeptical of you or your restaurant. With a properly executed new homeowners program, the clientele should mirror your best guest. Considering that they have no propensity to go anyplace else (because they haven't settled in enough to set habits), if you get them in the first time and they are "wowed" by you, that means that their chance of becoming a loyal guest is 300% better than somebody else (that you would have to steal away from another restaurant). Remember, the key to marketing is understanding human psychology and math. All marketing must be measured against the results it produces, and just like any other expense, if it can't carry its weight...get rid of it.

ACTION PLAN

1.   Find a reputable list broker and acquire a list of new homeowners in your area.

2   Develop a 3-step sequential mailer. Use Dan Kennedy's "Ultimate Sales Letter" as a guide to writing the best possible marketing pieces. For examples, go to TheFullRestaurantBook.com/ActionPlan

3   Implement the mailer…like Nike® says, "Just Do It!"™

BONUS STRATEGY

Be sure when you purchase your list, you are choosing people who have moved from outside the county. You don't want to mail to people who refinanced or moved two blocks down the road.

CHAPTER 3
Referrals: The Easiest New Guest to Sell
by Dean Killingbeck

Referrals are a great source for new guest acquisition. However, you'll notice I say a referral is the "*easiest* new guest to sell," not necessarily the *best*. Even though you have no control over who's coming in as a referral, remember…you have **zero cost** in getting them into your restaurant. So guess what? You can afford to weed out the ones that will never become good lifetime guests.

Let me give you an example of what I'm talking about. I have a client who owns a very upscale restaurant. In fact, his demographics look like this: his best guest has an average household income of $100,000, is between the ages of 45 and 65, owns their own home, and subscribes to a fine dining or wine magazine. That's the "face" (so to speak) that he puts on his best guest…Gray Hairs (or thinning hairs like me), with money to spend. By the way, his restaurant is a bistro with a wine bar.

He has referral reward systems in place (notice I said "systems") that reward both his wait staff and existing guests. I'll explain both systems in detail, but I wanted to point out that he has **more than one system** to attract referrals.

Employee Referral System

The first referral system that my client uses is an Employee Referral System. His wait staff/employees receive four referral gift cards each month which they are encouraged to hand out to anyone they want. Well, almost anyone (he's smart, not crazy!). The employees are asked to give them to people they do business with, friends, and even acquaintances. The one stipulation given is that they only hand out the referral cards to people who will be dining at the restaurant for the *very first time*. In other words, no one should be coming in for the second time with a freebie. All cards handed out have the employees' names on them, along with pertinent information: what is the offer? For example; a free entrée up to $25), hours of operation, expiration date, etc.

At the end of the month my client scans through the redeemed cards to make sure each employee is handing out their cards, and also to see exactly how well the restaurant fared at acquiring new guests. He then uses that information to determine exactly what his ROI was for that month.

NOTE: You must brutally and honestly measure and track your results.

So here's the real deal. As with any new guest acquisition system, you must be brutal as you measure and track these forms of incentives because they can be abused. Do I sound like a broken record? Good! Because it's an important fact! Frankly, you should *expect* them to be abused, and also be ready and able to deal out swift and appropriate action to the individuals who abuse them. What do I mean? "You fire their butts" if an employee abuses the system. Why? If they're abusing the system, they're basically stealing money out of your and your family's pocket. My mother's favorite saying was, "Don't cross over that bridge unless you want to reach the other side." In other words, if you aren't willing to fire an employee who abuses the referral card system, then don't initiate the system in the first place. That's my little bunch of pertinent home-spun psychology.

Reward Your Employees. Anyways, back to the

system…post all of the results for each month, listing the employees' names and who came in with their cards, and dollars spent by the guests, and then name the employee with either the most guests who came in, or the most money spent (that's your call) as the Winner. Give the monthly winner a great bottle of wine (however, don't get caught supplying alcohol to minors…check ID!), free movie tickets for them and three of their friends, a night off with pay, $2 more an hour for a full day, etc.

Create Competition. One of my other clients used this same system as a contest by separating his employees into two teams. He used the contest during his typically slowest month of the year (this month could be different based on where your restaurant is located). Basically, how it worked was he gave all his employees ten gift certificates to pass out. The team members were encouraging each other, having a great time razzing the other team, and they all had a ton of fun. At the end of the contest, the "team" results were calculated and the winners got steak, while the losers got beans. The restaurant owner came out the REAL winner, with hundreds of new guests coming to his restaurant to "help" the employees' team win.

BONUS STRATEGY

Make your gift certificates look professional. Use high quality cardstock and, for heaven's sake, use full color. Any good printer can do the personalized printing of your employee's name on the front of the certificate. Also, don't forget to include all your contact information: hours of operation, address, phone number, website, map, and, of course a way to capture the visiting guest's information. See our website for more details at TheFullRestaurantBook.com/ActionPlan

Welcome Dr. Freud. Now let's talk about the whole psychology of this specific referral system! It's a feel good-feel good system. It makes the guest feel good because they get a free entrée...who doesn't love stuff for free? Also, it makes the employee feel good and gives them the recognition every employee seeks and craves.

How? Your employee handing out these gift certificates should be made to feel special whether they're a waiter, chef, bus-boy, hostess...whatever. No matter how busy your restaurant is, when a guest comes in with a referral gift certificate, be sure the employee who gave out the gift certificate gets the chance to say hello to his special guest before they leave.

Remember, that employee invited that guest into your establishment and the employee should thank them for coming in. Sure, it was a great offer for the guest, but your employee was the one that presented the gift. If you recognize the employee in a special way, then they will continue to invite more guests with your referral program!

Guest Referral System

The second referral system is executed by your existing guests. Ask your existing guests to "refer" you to a friend of theirs. You can do this simply by handing out gift cards very similar to the employee gift card, but have a space on the card where your guest can write their name and then pass it to a friend. You can offer your existing guest a free dessert for every new guest they refer.

Again, your existing guest feels special because when they refer a friend, they receive something for FREE, and the invited guest feels special because they get a FREE entrée. Of course, the number one thing you should focus on is getting the visiting guest to join your birthday club membership (or other loyalty program)...in other words, "Get their name!" Tackle them before they make it through the exit door and get their name and info.

Lure Them In With Free Food! Another way to execute an Existing Guest referral program is through an appetizer party. Basically, how that works is you take your typical slowest night of the week and invite your best 200 guests to stop by to enjoy free appetizers and non-alcoholic beverages. However, in order to be admitted to the party, they must bring a guest that's not already in your birthday club.

Put out some really great appetizers and WOW the newbies with your fantastic food! Some of my clients even combine a fund raiser with their appetizer party, so they can help a local charity or other cause that's big in the news! You may even wind up with some free advertising if the local newspaper or TV stations hear about it.

NOTE: Always be looking for something in the news – locally, nationally, or worldwide – that can give you a reason to throw a quick party and expand your in-house guest list.

Another spin on the appetizer party...you can even have a drawing where everyone enters their name for a chance to win a party for 8...a $400 value! (Your cost is only $120, but they don't need to know that, do they?) By doing so, you have everyone filling out the card with their name and address. And, if they purchase drinks, give them an extra entry for each drink purchase, so they have an increased chance of winning the drawing, and an increased bar tab!

When hosting special charitable events, sometimes other merchants will be willing to tag along on your ingenious marketing methods. Offer the names of the guests who participate as "trade" (so they can use the list in their marketing), but ONLY if they contribute something to your event that is of real value.

A hardware store could give you a gas BBQ grill, a grocery store could give you a $100 shopping spree, and a hair salon could give a free manicure and pedicure. I'm sure you get the idea, but it has to be something of value...no rubber ducky. They donate the prize and you get the credit!

Merchant to Merchant Referral System

The third referral system would be merchant to merchant where both of you agree to hand out valuable gift certificates to your guests to be used at the other merchant's business as a "Thank You For Doing Business" with you.

Example: The local hardware store. When the hardware store has a customer purchase, say $50 or more, they'll give that customer a $10 gift certificate to use at your restaurant as a "Thank You for your Business" from the hardware store. On the flip side, you can hand out $10 gift certificates to use at the local hardware store to your best clients as a "Thank You" for being a great guest. It's the "I scratch your back, you scratch mine" type of system. However, you need to have a few rules: only give each other 20 gift certificates a month (or whatever number of certificates that is appropriate for your arrangement so you're always getting the best guest).

NOTE: This is not meant to be handed out to every Tom, Dick, and Shirley…only to the "best guests." This is called "Affluent Marketing." For more on Affluent Marketing, see Dan Kennedy's new book , No B.S. Marketing to the Affluent.

Set stipulations on who can receive the gift certificates. If you only want people who spend over $100, be sure the hardware store is aware of your stipulations. Again, as you continue to get new guests coming in, keep track of your redemption numbers, the names of your new guests, and feel free to tweak the program as needed.

Charity Referral System

The fourth system is when you're contacted by the High School PTA, Band Club, Football Booster or some other club, asking for free stuff as a means of supporting their cause. Let them know you'll support them, but tell them you will do one better…give them ten $20 coupons but only charge them $5 each. They turn around and sell the certificates for face value ($20) and make a profit of $15 each, for a total of $150. Now, if they only want to sell the certificates for $10, they'll only make a profit of $50, but that's their call. If you want to sell them one hundred coupons (their cost $500), and they turn around and sell them for $20, they can make $1500, and you'd have 100 guests flooding your restaurant!

NOTE: These types of gift certificates don't have a huge redemption rate, with the normal breakage or unredeemed rate being between 20% - 28%, meaning you'll only have between 72-80% redeemed. The best part? You *bought* those new customers for $1.00 each! How? They come in with their $20 gift certificate. Because your food cost is only around 30%, you're basically giving them $6.00 worth of food for free. Since you were already paid (by the charity) $5 for each certificate, you're only "giving away" $1... and you now have the chance to make that new guest a "loyal guest!"

By now I'm sure you understand how important it is to have a system in place to continually get referrals from not only guests, but from your employees. However, let me give you a quick word of caution: you must be willing to track the numbers. Remember, it's all about ROI. You must get all your materials, emails, and all means of reaching your guests planned before you need to use them, because with charity events, it's all about timing. Don't come up with a charitable event and then try to implement everything in a hurry...by the time you figure it out, it's too late. You should even be small-talking other merchants and get them lined up before you need them to "donate."

ACTION PLAN

1. Get the PDF file of Referral Certificate and then develop one for yourself. Go to: TheFullRestaurantBook.com/ActionPlan for the referral certificate.

2. Decide on gifts for the employee who brings in the most referrals. This has to be a good gift, something that entices some competition...a cheesy $5 certificate to the local McDonald's (that was just a joke...no nasty emails please) isn't going to cut it. Figure out how much a lifetime guest is worth to you and base the prize on a percentage of that number. Introduce the system and then follow up with a

vengeance! Also, lay out all the ground rules and consequences in case someone cheats.

3. Get all of the necessary arrangements made with printers, email, and sponsors for potential charity events, so in case something news-worthy happens, you can act quickly while it's fresh in everyone's mind and they're looking for a way to help out a charity or cause.

CHAPTER 4
You Either Have Lifetime Guests...
Or You Have Acquaintances
by Dean Killingbeck

When consulting with restaurants, I always ask them one simple question, "As a restaurant owner, what do you consider is the most important asset in your restaurant?"

Almost every time I get answers like: location, building, staff, menu, and high-quality food. Very seldom do I get the correct answer: "My Guest List."

Frankly, without a guest list, a business owner really doesn't have a solid business. Why, you ask? Because all their guests are only "acquaintances." They feel free to come and go as they please and typically have no loyalty to the restaurant or its owner. However, if the restaurant has a guest list, the owner can invite them to come back again and again, making them feel special with the various offers (no matter how miniscule), creating loyalty, which in turn may end up saving the restaurant. Read the story below to see what I mean.

Rory Fatt, a marketing guru and owner of Restaurant Marketing Systems (and personal friend), told me about one of his clients who owed the IRS a huge bill. Fortunately for him, he also had a huge guest list. He wrote a letter describing his situation with the IRS and his major tax bill, made an irresistible offer to come into his restaurant to "help him out," and mailed it to everyone on his guest list. Quicker than you can say "Jack Be Nimble, Jack Be Quick" he had $16,000 in extra sales in the next two weeks, which ended up paying his elephant-sized tax bill and saving his restaurant from closing! Okay, so some of you are probably thinking that you would NEVER tell your guest list that you had tax problems. Well, guess what, Mr./Ms. High-and-Mighty? Almost EVERYONE has problems paying taxes and other excessive bills. His customers loved him, and the letter he wrote touched a nerve that spurred them into action. They showed their love, respect, and support by responding in droves to his plea and helping him by coming and eating so he didn't have to close his restaurant. He had two choices: get the money, or close up his restaurant.

Create Relationships. A guest list gives you the opportunity to create relationships with your guests, making them feel like part of your family. It also is a valuable tool to create the all important *loyalty* to your restaurant, especially if you "touch them" monthly with a personality-driven newsletter, but more about that in a later chapter. If your guest feels like they have a relationship with you, it's hard for the big chain restaurants to steal them away with their billion dollar advertising methods that bombard your guests daily. If your guests feel personally connected to you and your restaurant, they'll think twice about skipping over to the local big chain for a 2 for 1 deal, or whatever else the chain is pushing that month.

So, back to my favorite question…do you have a well-managed list of your existing guests that includes the following?

☐ First name and Last name (including spouse, if applicable)

☐ Mailing Address

☐ Email address

☐ Phone numbers, including home and cell

☐ Important dates: including birthdays, anniversaries, kids' birthdays, and when they became a guest (their "restaurant anniversary").

If you answered "Yes," then congratulations! In the following chapters, you're going to hear several ideas on how to create excitement for your guests and make your restaurant tons of cash! However, if you answered "No," then (watch out...here come my angry eyebrows again) Shame On You! In the following chapters, you're going to be kicking yourself because you can't implement the amazing money making ideas right away (by the way, if you can actually kick yourself...DANG! You're flexible!) BUT, because you're a great marketer-to-be...tomorrow you're going to begin compiling that list as soon as you get to work, right? (Just answer, "Yes, Sir!")

Also, if you don't have a guest list yet, to help you out, I'll explain the quickest and easiest ways to get that accomplished so you can stop stressing.

Setting Up Your New Guest List (or fixing a broken one!)

The best way to start a new guest list is to start! Now trust me, you don't need 14 hours of community college classes to make it happen. Heck, I'm an old farmer and even I can do it! Microsoft Excel is pretty much pre-installed on most computers running Windows. A basic spreadsheet program or a list management system you already are using should be fine as well. Not sure how those programs work? There is always a "Help" tab that will help you find answers to your questions, and if you have kids, grandkids, or neighbor kids, these days I think they learn how to do all that in 2nd grade! Ask around...I'm sure there's always an employee that will help you out as well. That being said, you'll want to construct your list using specific column headings. The column headings I recommend are:

First Name

Last Name

Street Address

City

State

Zip

Cell Phone

Home Phone

Email Address

Birthday
(only month and day)

Anniversary
(only month and day)

Date of First Visit

You can add more columns for special ideas that you have in mind, but these should always be included in a good guest list. Creating this list is simple and easy…inputting the available data will take time, patience, and discipline. Hire a high school kid… they're quick and efficient with computers, and also reasonably priced.

Start Collecting Information

Start by collecting information on your current clients and people you know personally. Some of that information (instead of contacting them to get it) can be found locally online with address directories, neighborhood directories, church directories, Facebook, clubs, etc. However, an easier way to get your list up and running is by using what you already have…employees that are out on the floor every day talking to your guests.

Your employees should be well trained to encourage guests to sign up for your Preferred Guest List. You don't have to use that exact title. In fact, you can choose to give your house list any name you want: i.e., "The Hot Topics," "Grandma's Gorgeous Guests," etc. You get the picture. But train your employees to explain the benefits the guest receives by having their name on your list (free entrées for their birthdays, special deals being offered only to guests on the guest list throughout the year, etc.).

BONUS STRATEGY

Be sure to let your guests know that their contact information will NEVER be shared with anybody else… GUARANTEED!

Double Reward For Sign-Ups. To get a jumpstart on building your list, here's a simple idea you can put to use immediately. In order to entice your guests to want to sign up for your guest list, you need to make it worth their while. Listen, you can't expect your employees to get excited about interrupting a guest's meal to ask if they want to sign up for a guest list because if they sign up, they can receive a Free Soft Drink. BORING! And heck, interrupting someone to offer them a free soft drink might get your employee loads of dirty looks, get them yelled at, lose them a tip, or even have a plate of food tossed at them! Do you think your staff will be excited about that? Heck No! Your employees will be more willing to pursue guests to sign up for your list if: 1) the reward to the **guest** is fantastic; and, 2) the reward you give to the **employee** is fantastic!

BONUS STRATEGY

Okay, you know the lifetime value of the guest is staggering, right? So I'm going to give you a few ideas to help grow your guest list, including Rewarding Your Employees. But, I'm also going to give you a warning...**Don't Be Cheap**! Give your wait staff bonuses for collecting information on your guests.

I have a client that gives $1 for each new guest the employee signs up, plus a $50 bonus each pay period to the employee who signed up the most guests! He posts the results every pay period, with the rewards given in cash in front of all the employees at the beginning of each shift. Why be so dramatic? This way, everyone sees the money the participating employees are getting. Want to hear the best part? After two pay periods of giving bonuses, my client found that the previously indifferent employees (as well as the least productive) became the ones that ended up being the most productive! Why? Money motivates! Dangle that $50 carrot, and you'd be surprised what can happen!

So, just like you have to dangle the carrot for your employees to participate, you have to dangle the carrot for your guests to participate as well. You can try promotions like the following: "Sign up for 'Raul's Rockin' Registery' and as our way of saying "Thank You," on top of all the great offers you'll receive throughout the year, you'll receive a $10 gift certificate to use on your **next visit!**"

How To Avoid Joe Shmoe. That's right...reward your guest for signing up with a $10 gift certificate. The kicker is that you **mail** that gift certificate to them. Why? This almost guarantees that they fill out their information completely and accurately. They **want** the certificate to be mailed to their house, so they're going to make sure that the address is correct. Also, feel free to ask them for their email, their phone (including cell), birthday and anniversary. Only ask for the month and day, so you're more likely to get responses.

Heck, if you have an employee with the right personality, your employee can ask the questions of your guests and complete the form for them...making it a pain-free, quick process, guaranteed to make the guest feel special.

Gather Information From...Where Else?
"The Information Highway"

You can also collect information on your website. However, like before...in order to avoid Joe Shmoe, let them know that you'll be mailing them their certificate instead of them being able to instantly download it from your site. If you do not already have a fully optimized website, with an "irresistible offer" for potential guests to "sign-up," that will be something you'll definitely want to make happen in the near future. It is beneficial to building your list and attracts a younger, more affluent clientele. I recommend only using a reputable web design and/or optimization service that has experience dealing with restaurants like yours. Ask to see their testimonials of satisfied independent owners like yourself and get a full, money back guarantee.

The business that I use and have been MORE than satisfied with and personally recommend is www.56Seconds.com. The assistance of an administrative assistant or staff person with an available 5-15 minutes a day can keep you fully up to date on all aspects of building your list, website, etc. Since you know the lifetime value of a guest; you will never begrudge the time, effort, and small expense of doing this.

Gather Information From What You Already Have

If you're utilizing one of the new guest acquisition systems discussed in Chapter 1 and 2, you should be provided with an Excel spreadsheet from your list broker containing full names, addresses and, if mailing a birthday campaign, birth months. You can simply cut and paste names from that list into your guest list as they come in to redeem their offers at your restaurant.

NOTE: Telephone numbers, emails, anniversaries and other information are typically not supplied with lists from a broker. Your staff must still obtain that information directly from the guest redeeming the gift certificate. That information can be obtained through your staff with simple on-site surveys, and cards convincing the birthday or new mover guest to join the house list, or the employee having that guest sign up to be on your guest list to receive more great offers throughout the year.

Different Ways Of Utilizing Your In-House Guest List

With your gorgeous, shiny new "guest list" at your fingertips (be it a list of one hundred or ten thousand), you can start controlling your newly developed "4 M's...Money Making Marketing Muscle." There are numerous ways that you can market to your list, with new methods being developed all the time. However, keep in mind...not all methods are created equal. Direct mail, email, phone calls (personal or pre-recorded "phone blasts") etc., are all tools available to you. Direct mail and email are the two biggest ways that restaurants are marketing their guest lists right now.

Using Emails and Direct Mail

As a rule, direct mail works best for acquiring new, highly qualified, first time guests. However, if you're trying to do something quick and fast with a "guest list" you already have rapport established, emails are a great option. Email blasts are reasonable, cheap, and a quick way to get your message out there when there's a time crunch. Here's an example:

> *"Our special today is going to be our world famous "pub burger," fresh fish, or porterhouse steak. Each meal will include a fresh, hand-sliced jumbo piece of homemade pie, just like Mom used to make. But you have to hurry! This offer expires tomorrow at 8:00 PM."*

You can email that message to your well-maintained list at mid-afternoon, and by evening, literally fill your restaurant up.

With direct mail, however, you'll need a little more planning. Plan out your holidays in advance for up to one year. We recommend that our clients try to at least keep and maintain a 6-month marketing calendar. There's Valentine's Day, Mother's Day, Memorial Day, Father's Day, 4th of July, etc., I could go on and on. Plus each month, you have guest birthdays and anniversaries (that you have on your guest list) to whom you should send a direct mail piece. Keep in mind the return on investment (ROI) will always be much higher getting current guests to return than when trying to acquire new guests through a purchased list.

When it comes to guest list birthdays and anniversaries, one of the key reasons I recommend sending a direct mail piece versus using email, is that the email response rate is low. I know email campaigns work…the problem is that only 1.5% to 2% of emails are actually opened by the intended recipients. Jammed email boxes, spam filters, bounce backs, bad email addresses, and blocked emails are all challenges that you're faced with when emailing.

When you use an email blast to reach your **entire** guest list, an "opened" rate of 2% is still a great return (2% of 1200 is still 24 families that respond, turning a slow night into a nice night). However, like with birthdays, when you're only targeting 100 people with a birthday that month, 2% of 100 is only 2 families that opened the email…therefore, you missed out on contacting the rest of the families to wish them a happy birthday. In those cases, direct mail wins every time, with an expected response rate of more like 25-35%, which basically gives you 25-35 families for a 44¢ stamp and a mailer…now that's some nice ROI!

NOTE: These "Special Events" can often be done with little or no discounting of high margin food items.

Looking at "The Big Picture" keep in contact with your guest list any way you can. Email is nice and convenient, but there are problems that tend to get worse over time. Also, it would be naïve to think that our Federal Government won't figure out a way to tax emails...if there's a way, they'll find it. Twitter or Facebook may be nice (see Chapter #8 on Facebook), but by themselves, they will not save a failing business or transform a good business into a great business. Like everything else, adapt and learn to work with what you have.

BONUS STRATEGY

As more rapport is developed, a creative restaurateur can really have fun doing some cool stuff. We've had clients use telephone blasts, coming from them personally, from the head chef, or even from celebrity impersonators.

A telephone blast is a prerecorded message that you "send" out to your guest list. Imagine "Elvis" inviting you to come in for a "hunka, hunka, peanut butter and banana sandwich" that is only offered on "The King's" birthday (which by the way, for you non-Elvis idolizers, is January 8th). Do you want more "unique holidays" like Elvis' birthday?

With a fantastic email campaign, you can fill your restaurant up with excited guests. With a properly structured direct mail campaign, you can expect excellent results. Your clients will learn to watch for your offers and be excited to open them when they come. Just like a kid getting a birthday card from grandma...if they know something great is going to be in that envelope or in that email, you can bet your fanny they're opening it!

Welcome Them Home

That's what it's all about. It doesn't matter if you send an email or a direct mail piece, Facebook or Twitter; it's about making your guests feel special and a part of your family. Give them that warm, cozy, "grandma feeling." That's what keeps them inside your iron fence and keeps them from straying onto a competitor's "lawn." If you believe in *secrets* (let's face it, what we don't know is a "secret"), then this *secret* of maintaining a guest list will help keep you from being a struggling restaurant owner and instead become a rich restaurateur.

Rewarding your guests on your house list could lift you from being a mediocre restaurant, to being so successful that your wait on Fridays and Saturdays has them out the door for over an hour. Best of all? Your guest is happy about waiting! Why? Because they know the wait is worth it, they love your restaurant, and they love you! Also, as an added bonus, you can start hiring only the best employees to work at your restaurant. How? Every employee wants to work at a booming restaurant, where the guests are happy (everyone knows the tips are huge when you have happy guests), the restaurant is always FULL so they can work full time, and the boss is well-liked and respected individual in the community.

NOTE: All media must be used…never rely on only one type of media. With today's technology, any and all methods of reaching your guests can and should be utilized and repurposed online with a variety of audio and video links. Most of this can be done at very little cost and the good news is…you don't have to do it all at once. Take one step at a time and the genesis of all your marketing will continue to grow as your experience, enthusiasm, and income soars.

One Last Bedtime Story.

I was told a story about a restaurant owner who turned a disaster (when his restaurant burned down to the ground) into a Godsend by using his guest list. It took him almost 2½ years to rebuild his restaurant because of insurance mumbo jumbo. Being a proactive person, he continued to send a newsletter every quarter. Each newsletter told his story and the progress that was being made, turning his "drama" into a story of "the little guy beating the odds" and the whole community started rallying around him and his efforts. When there was cause for celebration throughout the building process ("footings were poured!") he would erect a tent with a massive grill, fryers, and soda pop on ice and invite everyone to attend.

At one event, he had over 400 guests, munching on burgers, crunchy fries, and slogging down cokes. It was like the world's largest family reunion. In addition to his newsletter spurring attention and drawing guests during these events, he received a lot of radio, TV, and newspaper coverage (that was worth a small fortune). Nevertheless, the impetus for the whole thing was the faithful clientele with whom he took the time to nurture and share his story. Without the extra effort, he could have been known as "the guy whose restaurant burned down...Aw, shucks...guess we need to find another good place to eat." As it goes, when he had his grand opening, his guests not only waited out in the parking lot for two hours; heck, they waited for four hours. He actually had more business after he reopened and has retained that business still today.

Summing It All Up

The long term value of starting and cultivating your "guest list" can make your restaurant's value double or triple that of what a comparable restaurant is worth when (and if) the time comes for you to "cash out."

Personally, I would never buy a retail establishment or service industry that didn't have a guest list. Why? Because you're basically starting over from scratch and you might as well go out and build a brand new business. If the existing business doesn't have a guest list, you can't ask your best customers to walk through the door because: 1) you don't know who they are; and 2) you can't get in touch with them.

Without a house list, the value of any business is only that of the used equipment in the kitchen and the furniture in the dining room, which is not a whole lot. Also, with a good guest list, your restaurant can be impervious to all manners of financial disaster and you can sleep like a baby knowing you have the knowledge and tools in place to always survive and thrive in the restaurant business. Even moving to a different location could be a cause for a celebration and multiple week "events"…instead of a starting over from scratch set of expensive birthing pains.

With that said…Go work on your list!

ACTION PLAN

1.   Set up an Excel spreadsheet or use another CRM (customer relations management) system to begin your guest list.

2.   Start collecting names and information.

CHAPTER 5
Holiday Marketing
Put the Fun Back In Your Sales...
And A Whole Lot of Money in Your Pocket
Fun Marketing, Using Holidays!!!
by Dean Killingbeck

In the first three chapters, we discussed New Guest Acquisition. In Chapter 4, we talked about managing a guest list and why it is so important. Now, we will take this chapter and show you how to use that guest list to make you tons of money by marketing to those existing customers and having a system in place to get those guests to come back. They must make your restaurant a habitual place to visit. Your guest's car must practically drive itself to your restaurant without any driver. We call that a "habit."

NOTE: Existing Guests are the easiest and best customers to sell. They know who you are and they like your restaurant, your food, and staff...so all you have to do is make them an irresistible offer and a give them a reason to come running back!

This is going to be a busy chapter, so get your highlighters primed, grab a pen, and a pad of paper. You're going to get some wild ideas to double your profits that will begin bouncing around your brain and keep you up at night figuring how to implement another money making strategy!

One of the key ingredients of my "Secret Sauce of Marketing" (every chef has a secret sauce, why shouldn't I?) is to be fun and entertaining whenever possible. My mentor (and friend) Bill Glazer, recently wrote a #1 Best Seller called *Outrageous Advertising That's Outrageously Successful*. Every restaurant owner (if you're planning on doing any type of marketing) should own this book. I'll even go out on a limb and offer the readers of this book, a 100% money-back guarantee on Bill's book...it's that good! If you can't find one useful strategy to use, just send me a note and I'll refund the purchase price. Bill Glazer does a lot of things outrageously, to get attention, and since we're talking about having fun with our marketing, the book is certainly a "must read." It's a great reference manual where you can flip through to find just one outrageous advertising idea you can instantly use, like searching for recipes in a cookbook.

Holiday Marketing

To help make marketing FUN, it's good to have a "hook" or what we call a "reason why." Holidays are a great place to start... there are so many "holidays" that you could find one for virtually every day of the year, no exaggeration. Everybody knows about Mother's Day, Valentine's Day, Fourth of July, President's Day (almost all furniture stores have a President's Day sale!)...all of these are wonderful "hooks" and "reasons why." Done correctly, like the way we teach you in this book (that's me braggin'!) and through our courses and seminars, you can make tens of thousands of extra dollars every year of pure profit, cash money!

However, in this chapter, I want to take you to a whole new level of success, making you truly independently wealthy with a set of marketing systems that can be turned on and off like a faucet, producing consistent cash flow at will, while building into your business the occasional "Slack Adjuster." Slack Adjusters are big paydays that produce inordinately high profits in a short period of time. Think of a toy manufacturer and their "slack adjusters." Typically it's a high priced toy, such as those battery operated toy cars, Jeeps, and 4 wheelers that they make for $100 and sell for

$500. The profit structure is high. Do you have any slack adjusters built into your marketing program that are high margin for your empty table downtimes? Holiday Marketing can help.

The foundation for creating a "holiday" mailer always starts with an interesting "hook" (reason why) marketing ploy and, of course, an excuse to have fun. Holidays (both real and fabricated) are a key ingredient to producing a daily and weekly source of more business through your front door. Don't think you have to stick to "real" holidays...how about Broccoli Day, Kohlrabi Day, Dog Day, or Chester's Cheese Day? The only thing that limits the amount of holidays you can celebrate is your imagination. Also, all those "Hallmark Holidays" that are pushed on us (i.e., Secretary's Day, Teacher's Day, Grandparent's Day, Boss' Day)...can finally be put to good use. The one thing I want you to remember throughout this chapter is that you should implement your holiday marketing during the slowest time of *your* year, or *your* slowest time of the month.

Wherever you're located in the world, there are typically one or two consistently slow months of the year in your area. In the US, if you're located in the North, it's usually the wintertime; if you're in the Deep South (or you're a "snowbird" destination), it's usually in the summer. Therefore, strategize how to make yourself so exciting that you stand out from the rest of the crowd when things are slow. At a time when everyone else around you is taking a 20% to 35% dip in their income because of the "slow time," your cash flow is consistent because of the systems that you have in place to keep your regular customers coming back!

Remember, plan out your holidays in advance for up to a year and strive to keep and maintain a 6-month marketing calendar. Keep in mind the return on investment (ROI) will always be much higher getting current guests to return than when trying to acquire new guests through a purchased list.

When starting any marketing campaign, it's helpful to have a mental picture of the person you're selling to. The great copywriter, John Carlton has a story of who we all sell to... he calls it the "Somnambulant Sloth": a complete blob, just sitting there, unthinking and unmotivated to do any real thinking. I picture Homer Simpson, beer in one hand, donut in the other, trying to figure out how to juggle the TV clicker without putting the beer or the donut down. When hunger for real food finally reaches his brain, the challenge you face as a marketer is to overcome Homer's urge to put something in the microwave, or go to the place "everybody" else goes to. What can you offer Homer to get him to come to YOUR restaurant? That answer, my friend...is the key to a great marketing system!

In the following chapters, we will be looking at ways, or lures, that you can use to get guests into your restaurant. Some will work for you, some may not, but it's a collection of ideas that you can build off of.

No Peeking

No Peeking is one of my favorites because it's the perfect antidote for cyclical sales that ebb and flow and wreak havoc with your cash flow, and subsequently your mood. Just like your restaurant experiences "downtimes," it also has reliable "uptimes." We typically see a lot of our clients having steady, increased business during the end of the year (typically November and December) where their place is packed. However, every year, there is this month called January (I bet you've heard of it), when lots of people are "partied out" and our clients' business drops like a lead balloon. A No Peeking campaign is a great way to "fix" that.

No Peeking is a simple bounce back piece that is a fun way to get guests involved and excited to come back to your restaurant. Generally, it's a special, sealed, color envelope (we like Red for Christmas, Green for St. Patrick's Day, etc.) that you give your guests when they're packed into your restaurant during your "busy time," and in order for them to "play," they have to COME BACK to your restaurant during the dates that YOU specify on the envelope (typically you want them to come back during your slowest month). One extra bonus is that since you're "handing" it to them, you don't have to pay for postage…a big money-saver. It's a lot of fun.

Here's how the program works:

Your guest comes into your restaurant and has a meal. When the server brings the bill to the table, they also bring along a No Peeking envelope. On the outside of the sealed envelope, you'll describe five or six special gifts with "teaser text" stating everyone is guaranteed to win one of the prizes listed. The rule is they cannot open the envelope until they come back, and your server has to open it for them (so no one cheats). If they do open it, the offer is invalidated; hence, "No Peeking."

The server asks the guests if they would like to participate in the No Peeking program for a chance to win a $100 gift certificate (or whatever you choose as the highest gift) to the restaurant. The only thing the guest has to do is bring the unopened envelope back to the restaurant during the dates on the front of the envelope (ex., if you're handing them out in December, they need to come back between January 1st and January 31st). There is no other

60

obligation from the guest, making it an easy program to implement. When the guest comes back to your restaurant (REPEAT VISIT!!!) with their unopened No Peeking envelope, they show it to the server (before they order) and they are allowed to open it at that time and use their "prize" during that visit.

Wanna hear something outrageous? You're going to find that 35% to 40% of the guests that receive a No Peeking envelope come back in to your restaurant during the time specified. Are you starting to see how this can benefit you and give you a big jump in business when you want to see it most?

There are a few tricks used when implementing the No Peeking program, the most important is to TRAIN your staff on how to hand out the envelopes with excitement! You can't experience the jump in business if nobody is playing! Secondly, carefully strategize your gifts. As stated before, five or six gifts are listed on the envelope and everybody is guaranteed to win something. Be sure that your most expensive gift is something that will get "Homer" off of the couch. We've had clients give away 47" flat screen TVs, catered Super Bowl parties for 30 guests, $100 gift certificates to their restaurant, etc. The rest of the prizes are of lesser value, with the smallest prize being really cheap.

BONUS STRATEGY

Have a really cheap prize on your envelope (i.e. Free Fountain Drink) and **don't print** any certificates with that prize. Why list a cheap prize on the envelope and not print any winners? Face it...the general public has been "trained" to anticipate winning the lowest prize because they're used to "cheap" marketing ploys that tout great prizes yet don't follow through, or they go unawarded. The problem is that there is always a low value prize that EVERYONE wins.

Well, not at your place! A few will receive the big, nice prizes (which is great because they'll talk about it for years and you can even put their names and pictures in a newsletter and use it in other marketing), and hundreds will win your mid-price items and still spend lots of money on your menu. It's very smart psychology because everyone wants to feel special winning something and NOT winning the cheapest prize helps with that! So, even if your 2nd to cheapest prize isn't anything special, the guest will still think they came out ahead, because they'll think, "WOW! I didn't win the cheapest prize!"

When you have your envelopes printed, you'll also need to figure out how many of each prize you want printed to be inserted into your envelopes. You should base that on how much you are willing to give away to get as many people back into your restaurant. Let's say you had 2,000 envelopes printed. I recommend a few top prize winners (i.e., $100 or $50 gift certificates), and, depending on your offers, percentages for the rest, with the two lowest prizes receiving the bulk of the printing (except the "cheapest, which you'll print none of).

There is an example on our website
TheFullRestaurantBook.com/ActionPlan

So, with No Peeking, everybody is a winner! The program costs you only pennies, and you get to reap the thousands of extra dollars "bouncing back" because of a simple envelope. It's great to have a 30-40% return rate but the program is still profitable even if only 10% are redeemed. Of course, once you become "sold" on this, each year you'll strive to reach the 100% rate, like the rest of us – educating your staff to get excited in promoting the program will help increase your return rate!

Various Contests

More fantastic, fun stuff you can have ongoing with your monthly new movers, birthday, and "no peeking" programs... are contests. Contests are fun, engaging programs that provide great interest and an endless source of opportunities for you to work with. A restaurant contest can be based on some variable of skill, luck, or a combination of the two. Contests are great because they create anticipation, excitement, and encourage frequent visits to your restaurant. They can also be a lot of fun for you, your staff, *and* your guests.

My preferred contests are centered on an event. For example: the NCAA Basketball Playoffs, this crazy football game called "Super Bowl," or other sporting event finals are the perfect basis for contests.

BONUS STRATEGY

This can also be done with local sports teams: the local high school's football playoffs, basketball playoffs, etc.

Start your contest six weeks before the season ends and continue through playoff time. Every guest receives an entry into your drawing each time they dine with you during the contest period. There can be first, second, and third place winners, as well as a conciliation prize. Imagine a first place winner getting a "Never Wait Pass" so they can move to the front of the line whenever they come to your restaurant. Second place could win free desserts for a year; third place could win free soft drinks for a year...the possibilities are endless. And, everyone is a winner! Send all those "losers" a $5 gift certificate to use at your restaurant during the next four weeks.

To help you acquire a big house list fast, get your guests motivated and have a contest giving away a high definition flat screen TV. Now before you think I'm crazy, or think this is "too expensive," let me pull you out of your comfort zone and push you into the "zone" of making a lot of money without spending a ton. First off, the TV doesn't need to be enormous...a 42" flat screen HD TV can be purchased nowadays for less than $600. Now, if you get 2,000-3,000 entries over a period of a few months, that breaks down to paying (or better said, "investing") $.30 per name. That $.30 you invested acquired the name, address, and email from somebody who has been to your restaurant and spent their hard-earned money. Now you're armed with the contact information from quality clientele added to your "house list."

Contests are a great way to generate excitement and boost your sales. Just be sure that you're giving away something desirable: TVs, iPods, food, etc.

For example, a friend and good client of mine owns Alfie's Restaurant down in Florida. It's a great fish place that's been around for 26 years, and he has served close to one million fish dinners. He decided to create a "Millionth Fish Plate" contest. He wrote a letter that said, "Hey. It's Fish Day and we're getting close to selling our one millionth fish dinner. Come on in for your chance to win fabulous prizes." He actually put a rubber fish in the mailer with a letter explaining everything about it. Then, the guests

64

came in with their rubber fish, and they got to fish in his little pond. Instead of the typical ducks in the pond, he had plastic fish in the pond with prizes attached to them. When they pulled a fish out of the pond, they won free appetizers, free drinks, and much more. Plus, if they happened to order the millionth plate of fish, they won a bunch of grand prizes.

You can also tie contests to "holidays," like best Halloween costume, or a 1950's or 1960's dress up weekend. Music selections paired with certain foods can enhance events like Luau's, Sock Hops, etc. that you've planned. Market these events to your "house list," achieve media attention with press releases, and use a contest to gain so much attention, it'll make your competitor green with envy. Armed with your knowledge of lifetime value (LTV) and the use of "bounce back" pieces like the "no peeking" program, you will, in short, turn your ordinary business into an extraordinary money making machine.

Voting contests are another way to bring in business and keep your guests interested in your restaurant. Family oriented restaurants can display a wall of photos containing pictures of their guests' "Cutest Dogs." Tally up the voting results at the end of the contest and display a winner. Have a "Coloring Contest" and display kids' coloring skills with the winner displayed proudly at the end of the contest, and so on. Of course everyone wins some type of prize.

Events and contests can also be built around special occasions that are unique to you and your business. The anniversary of when your restaurant was established, was renovated, your personal birthday, your marriage anniversary, or something to honor a local charity or cause. These events can be small or big and may even include large capacity tents erected outside your business with a band, DJ, etc., with contests tied in to facilitate building your most valuable asset…your house list.

Puzzle Mailer Contest

A great gimmick that always works is a puzzle mailer using direct mail. Basically, the process entails purchasing two identical puzzles. The number of pieces for the puzzle should correspond to your house list, i.e., if you have 500 in your guests list, buy a 500 piece puzzle, and so on. The first puzzle is assembled entirely and displayed in your restaurant. The catch? You leave out 10-12 pieces and number the blank spaces and assign a gift to each number.

Using the second puzzle, you mail one piece to each person on your house list with an accompanying letter. The letter explains that if your guest brings in the puzzle piece to your restaurant, they can "compete" to win one of the prizes available by seeing if their puzzle piece fits into one of the blank spots. While they're there, the majority will have dinner…note this is at regular menu prices, no discounting required since the majority of your guests won't win!

As an incentive for the guests that didn't win to come back an additional time, offer all "losers" a bounce back certificate good for $5 towards their next visit. At $.44 for the stamp, price of the envelope, two pieces of paper, one or two certificates (depending on whether or not they were winners) and a puzzle piece, your cost is just a little over a dollar per letter to bring in a ton of business!

So get your thinking cap on, visit the website, and start your Holiday/Fun Marketing today!

ACTION PLAN

1. Look at last year's sales and determine your two slowest months.

2. Decide on whether you want to celebrate a holiday or an event.

3. Choose the method you're going to use to reach your guests. I recommend the following:

    a. Newsletter

    b. E-Mail

    c. Direct Mail

    d. Word of Mouth

    e. Publicity (only if it's a "cause")

4. Write your copy, decide on your prizes and then IMPLEMENT THE PROGRAM!

CHAPTER 6
A Done-For-You Kid's Club Marketing System to Get More Families Coming Into Your Restaurant!
by Dean Killingbeck

Smart restaurant operators know that when families go out to eat, more often it's the kids that are choosing the restaurant. In fact, across the board, kids have more and more purchasing power on where the family spends its money. It used to be, in the past, the most effective way to sell to children was to target them through their parents. Nowadays, however, the opposite is true. Children are the focal point for intense marketing programs seeking to influence billions of dollars of annual family spending. This year alone, according to the National Restaurant Association, children *under the age of 12* will *directly influence* the household spending of over $600 BILLION dollars! No wonder McDonald's®, and Burger King® have had increasing sales even in our slow economy.

Hitting Your Target

Marketing your restaurant to kids is a smart business move. I'm not referring to just a simple "Kid's Menu" distinction. What you really need for your restaurant is a complete and standout kid's marketing system to keep the families coming back. If your restaurant offers a memorable, engaging experience for the kids, and you continue to market directly to them, you will immediately reap the financial reward because you will have created "Loyalty" that can last the child's lifetime. "Daddy, I want to go to (insert your restaurant's name)", could be the sweetest words ever spoken. In other "sweet" words... GET THE KIDS!!!

Stop and think about it...what has Las Vegas done in the past

10 years? They're trying to make Vegas a "family-friendly" vacation spot! They've installed pirate ships that sink, roller coaster rides at the top of buildings, light shows, "enchanted" gardens with trees that speak, etc. Why go to all that trouble and spend all that money? Because if a family only takes one vacation a year…Vegas wants to be in the running as that destination!

So, if it's good enough for "Sin City," then you can "bet" it will work wonders for your restaurant (I couldn't resist the gambling reference)! Why not put in a fishing pond for kids 12 and under so they can go fishing for a prize…have a tub that they get to pick-out of…like the old rubber ducky game or the wall of kid's art, etc.

But just like when marketing to adults, your restaurant must give kids a reason to want to come back. If you don't stay in touch with the children directly, through your marketing (remember to use your list), you'll lose their interest, and their family's money!

If you think adults have a short attention span when it comes to a marketing message, imagine marketing to a child! Kids are always on the look out for the next, best, shiny object. If you're not making a connection and staying at the center of their thoughts, they'll be eating another Happy Meal® when Mom or Dad asks them, "Where do you want to eat tonight?" Don't lose out on your share of the family dining dollars because you don't know how to market to their kids.

In today's world, implementing a successful kids' program moves beyond a cup full of crayons and a slice of pepperoni pizza. A kid's menu alone, regardless of how good it is, does not guarantee repeat family visits; neither does a single, stand-alone promotion such as "Kids Eat Free On Tuesday Nights." The kids don't see any benefit in whether or not they have to pay...they NEVER have to pay (mommy and daddy do, with the never-ending supply of FREE money that comes out of that funny machine at the bank when their parents put in their "secret" card).

Today's kids are much more sophisticated (I'll use that word instead of what I was really thinking), and expect more from restaurants. Remember, kids are literally "running" a lot of households and if you're a parent (and heck, even if you're just breathing), I'm sure you've seen it happen quite frequently.

So, without being crass, why don't we take advantage of that *"trend"* and use it to our advantage. Certainly, both parents and restaurants are ready to move children's restaurant experiences to the next level. Having a complete Kid's Club Marketing System that encourages repeat business is the answer.

Satisfying Everyone

With all the studies being done on the importance of a family eating dinner together, an important strategy is: focusing on the family and the "family dining" experience. A good marketing message that resonates with parents will stress ideals that strengthen the family bond. More households have both parents working, and parents are more willing to spend money on a "family-focused experience" at your restaurant. This may go back to the guilt that parents feel over working too much and not spending enough time with their kids.

When families go about choosing where to eat, the common scenario has parents thinking about which restaurants are convenient, child-friendly...while the kids are thinking about restaurant options that are fun and "what's in it for me!"

Recognizing the power children yield and understanding that with children come families (and bigger checks) to your restaurant, is important to increasing your sales. Getting more repeat visits, and as a result more business, is what we're talking about and the easiest way to do that is with your marketing. Treat kids as "Little Adult" guests, and they will soon become your restaurant's Super Consumers into actual adulthood! Teach your employees to ask the child for their name and then have a special question for them, i.e., "What's Your Favorite Color?" No matter what the child answers, they're a winner ("Yes! That was the color of the minute!") and then give them a token they can use. Nobody is a loser!

Marketing For Your Future

Marketing directly to kids is also a good way of building future business for your restaurant. It's never too early to start building your database of future guests for your restaurant, by starting a lasting relationship with the kids that will yield consistent sales throughout the years. Kids grow up and have two choices: become your guest, or leave your restaurant for your competition. According to the Retail Association, in 2009, teenagers between the ages of 12 and 19 spent over $172 Billion. If you develop a strong relationship with them early in their "teen-hood," you have less chance of losing them in their adult life.

So How Do You Create a Great Kid's Program?

You need to start by creating a "Family Dining Experience" instead of the typical scenario where the kids just color and the parents ignore them. If everyone interacts as a family, the better the dining experience, and the happier they are (and as a result you perpetuate repeat visits). How do you accomplish this family interaction? Through interactive, fun games and questions in which the family can all participate together using an activity placemat. The placemat also contains your customized Kids Menu, so there is no need to have a separate Menu (decreasing your costs).

Pay close attention to the creation of your kids menu and make it as fun as possible. Today's children have more "sophisticated" tastes than just chicken fingers and French fries. Give them some variety and healthy choices to create a successful menu. Heck, schools are pushing good nutrition down their throats on a daily basis, and heaven knows, with our obese nation, we all need it! Also, include the application for your Kids Club on the placemat with a description of how the program works. Then ask a couple questions that are designed to start your Kid's Club database.

The Birthday Card

The number one reason for dining out, especially for children, is birthdays! Now there's a special word... Birthday! Everyone celebrates them and you know for certain that kids don't come alone! Kid's club members should receive a full color birthday card during the month of their birthday (I'll have more about that in a minute).

Personalize it just for them with a note from your restaurant, and a certificate to return to the restaurant during their birthday month for a Special FREE Birthday Dinner and Treat. The great thing about kid's birthdays is that they are bringing the whole family with them. Sometimes that includes extended family and/or family friends as well! As an incentive to increase the number of guests, you can have a special offer in your note for the birthday child: Bring more than three guests with you and receive 1 Kid

Buck for every additional guest (I'll explain what a Kid Buck is a little later)! This is a brilliant way to encourage more guests to come to your restaurant. A little sneaky? Possibly... Inventive, Creative, and Imaginative? You Betcha!

The Welcome Package

What child gets excited when the mail comes and there is something addressed to him or her personally? Answer: they ALL do. As soon as a child signs up for your Kid's Club, they should receive a "Welcome Package" addressed directly to them from your restaurant. Inside, put a letter from your restaurant, personalized to the child, welcoming them as a new member of your kid's club program. Explain the benefits and what they will receive as a member, and include 1 Kid's Buck to start them off and get them excited about the program.

If you can wing it, include a personalized ID card with your restaurant's logo and Kid's Club information on it. Also, try adding a small toy to make your package stand out. "Bulky Mail" is a favorite with kids, and they LOVE to get *stuff* (like cheap plastic frogs that they can play with (from Oriental Trading Co. for $0.035 each).

Most importantly, include a certificate to "Buy Mom and Dad Dinner!" from your restaurant. This makes the child feel important and grown up, because they can take Mom and Dad out and buy them dinner for a change. It also makes the parents feel good about the program and drives business back into your restaurant immediately. Use full-color certificates and customize them to your restaurant. We are seeing on average between 50 and 80% redemption rates on these type of certificates. Why is it so high? Because they are your existing customers and their kids are anxious to bring their parents back into the restaurant because *they* are the ones that received the award and *they* usually determine/decide where to eat!

Kid's Bucks

Your restaurant's Kid's Bucks are the *foundation* of your Kid's Club program. These Bucks are designed to get the Kids to want to return to your restaurant again and again. Use customized Kids Bucks as an award by handing out to kids when they come in to eat. Restaurants already using this program are being very creative in what their Kid's Bucks can be redeemed for, and how the kids can get more Kid's Bucks. To make the most of the program, it's best to display the prizes and/or rewards to get kids excited about accruing more Bucks.

For example, Greg Evans from Alfie's Restaurant is giving away a Bike for only 100 Kid's Bucks. He is displaying the bike in the restaurant, so all the kids can see what they can buy with their Bucks. The bike cost Greg only $75, and if the child has to dine at his restaurant between 30 and 60 times to acquire 100 Kid's Bucks, Greg knows his Return on Investment (ROI) for that bike is huge!

Other restaurant owners are displaying a treasure chest of small toys that the kids can choose from after collecting only 10 Kid's Bucks. By giving out the Kid's Bucks for every visit you give instant gratification and create a habit. This helps when the parents ask their kids where they want to eat tonight, the reply will always be *your* restaurant...because they want more of your Kid's Bucks and prizes! You can choose a variety of ways to promote your Kid's Bucks and encourage repeat visits...giving a buck every time the child dines at your restaurant and show their personalized ID

Card, if they enter your coloring contest, if they show their report card with good grades, and so on…the possibilities are endless.

In summary, to have a successful Kid's Club, you can make it as easy or as sophisticated as you determine necessary. However, a few strategies that must be followed are:

1. Give the child something of value and personalize mail directly to that child.

2. The child should receive an offer with a newsletter every other month, with monthly newsletters being ideal.

3. You can go online to find out all sorts of information about Kid's Clubs, or hire a service to have it all Done For You. One of my favorites, and a Kid's Club Guru, is Michael Thibault of www.RestaurantKidsClub.com. Refer to the resources section in the back of this book for more contact information.

WARNING: This Last Chapter About Offline Marketing May Upset You, Try Your Patience, Or Cause You To Go Into Anaphylactic Shock (That's Really Painful!)

CHAPTER 7
Stop Being An Advertising Victim
by Dean Killingbeck

The new emerging economy will offer more opportunities and greater return for the nimble, accurate thinking people in the food service business.

For those unwilling to face-the-facts & step up to the plate, their business life expectancy isn't long at all. – Dean Killingbeck

Because I'm such a nice guy (I'm sure you've heard that)…I must give you the secret that other so-called "Advertising Gurus" fail to mention (especially when they're trying to sell you thousands of dollars worth of marketing). Actually, there are two secrets, and you've heard about both in previous chapters, but they are well worth repeating. First, not all guests are created equal and second, you must brutally and honestly measure all marketing. Okay, I also have to add a Third secret (because I'm crazy like that)… All Marketing is Math (ROI vs. LTV).

So I ask you…have you ever felt like an advertising victim? We all become "victims" when we're sold by someone — even if that "someone" is ourselves. You think you should use or try a strategy that sounds like a winner, but in the end, the only person who has "won" is the person who sold you the strategy!

Here's an example: some local sales rep shows up at your place of business and pitches you some whiz-bang advertising deal that is going to "give your restaurant phenomenal exposure and have people flocking in!" When the rep explains it, the idea seems to make so much sense (like you're finally playing in the big leagues). So you reach down for your big old business checkbook, neatly fill in all the right numbers, and sign it with a flourish. With a firm hand, you crease and tear out the perforated sheet with a resounding "zzz...zzzz...zip" and hand it over to the sales rep. He smiles, shakes your hand, congratulates you on making such a good decision and walks out the door (with YOUR fat check in HIS wallet...no wonder he's smiling!).

You felt confident as you wrote the check, but as you watched him stroll out the door, there's this empty, nagging feeling of dread..."*Did I make the right decision? Will I ever get my money back? Did I just become an Advertising Victim? Was that guy wearing a toupee?*" (I'm just kidding...Please...no emails from the follically challenged...I'm a member of that club myself! I just wanted you to get rid of that empty nagging feeling!)

A Victim's Tale (well, almost!). Don't let yourself become an advertising victim! As easy as that is to say, it still happens to the best of us. A few years back, a friend of mine, Sterling, opened *The Purple Mushroom*. It was a restaurant in my hometown of Howell, Michigan, niched to serving breakfast and lunch. He is a wonderful chef; warm and gracious, always greeting his guests with a warm smile, and he had a slew of delectable dishes that made your mouth water just reading the menu! I liked him and his restaurant so much that we ended up becoming business partners, but not before he almost made the worst decision of his marketing career. Let me explain...

Shortly after he had opened his business, and before we really got to know each other, I had stopped in for lunch. He greeted me and asked if I wanted to hear about "this great advertising deal" he just got (he knew I was a marketer and that I wrote about things of this nature, speaking around the country). I think he wanted to impress me just a little, and I admired his enthusiasm, so I invited him tell me all about it. He took a deep breath and said the stupidest thing I ever thought he could've said: "I think what I'm going to do is this...I have a chance to bring out the local radio station, WHMI, here in Howell. They'll put up a remote site and they'll spend the whole day Saturday and Sunday broadcasting live from my restaurant! Everybody will love it!"

Not wanting to tell him he was crazy, I said, "Wow, that's cool! So, what's that going to cost you?" He responded, "Well, it's going to cost me $6,000!" and I almost fell out of my chair. So I *had* to ask, "So, give me an idea of how many *new people* you think that'll bring through your doors." He answered, "Well, I don't know... I'd expect at least three to five hundred new people."

"Well," I said, "I think you're being really optimistic, so I'll go with the conservative '300' number. So, three hundred people divided into $6,000, means you're spending $20 a person to get them into your place." Now, in my eyes, that's a lot of money and it's not very accurate, considering it's based on a lot of *assumption* on his part. I asked him if he had the extra money to spend and he stammered and confessed that he didn't. However, they offered him a payment program he could put on his credit card (eeeeek!). He was planning on paying his credit card off with the profits he was going to make on this "big extravaganza." Besides being a great chef, another one of Sterling's tremendous talents is the ability to "read peoples faces." He stared at me intently as he could see the doubt in my eyes. He then asked, "Do you know of a less expensive way that will help me grow my business and not put me in debt?"

So, I cleared my throat and offered my advice. "How about this? Why don't you go around and put door hangers on the doors of everybody within a mile radius? You are surrounded by thousands of upscale homes and condos...offer them one free breakfast or free lunch, on you, as part of your Grand Opening Celebration. Free, no cost, no obligation!"

His face lost all expression, so I continued, "Consequently, they'll bring other people to eat with them. You pack the place and you get to be the hero." I explained that on the back of the door hangers there would be a place for them to fill in their name, address, and other information in order to receive their free entrée. The best part was, for a couple hundred dollars, he could get a few thousand door hangers printed. More importantly, he'd be able to measure his ROI and he'd know exactly how many customers the promotion brought in, because he'd have the redeemed door hanger tags with their information!

Better still, the wholesale cost of their one free meal would be $4 max, which means altogether, he'd end up spending a lot less than the $20/person the radio gig was going to cost. The door hanger would be valid only for the people who brought them in, with the vast majority of people not coming in alone. Their "friend's" plate of food, coffee, fountain drinks, etc. would be charged full price, offsetting the out of pocket cost of the "free" meal. At the end of the weekend or month, he would have acquired hundreds of new customers, with their full contact information, given them a "bounce back" certificate to encourage them to come back, and still make a profit. Needless to say, he smiled, took my suggestions, and implemented my plan with great success. He spent $432 on 1000 door hangers and got a 20.7% response. With an average ticket sale of $6.37 (remember, he's a breakfast and lunch establishment), he grossed approximately $1,320. Fast forward a year and a half…we were having lunch and he said to me, "Do you realize that if I would have done the WHMI radio station extravaganza, I'd just be making the final payment now? I can't believe that I even thought of doing that."

NOTE: All Marketing is about the math…you must be able to brutally and honestly measure your ROI!!

So, that's what I mean when I say Don't Be An Advertising Victim. I don't think any of us entrepreneurs can honestly say that we haven't been an advertising victim one time or another. And, it's truly not our fault! Why? Because we're not trained on what good marketing is and how we can brutally and honestly measure our results to *know* what good marketing is. Basically, the only thing we have as a reference point is what we see other business people doing. With that said we *do* have to take responsibility for our actions and from this point forward, become brutally honest with measuring the costs of our advertising. Now don't misunderstand me…I'm not suggesting that you only take the cheapest route and don't invest generously in marketing and advertising. In this economy it's imperative that you do.

However, I am saying be brutally honest with your ROI. With a good understanding of how to be brutally honest in calculating and then measuring your returns, you can stop being a victim. It's as simple as accurately looking at the real costs, or investment, and what the anticipated and acceptable rate of return can and should be. When you see what actually works, then it's just a matter of repeating as much of it as you can, as frequently as you can. If I asked any owner what their food cost is, they can tell me to the

80

penny. But, when I ask the same question about marketing, I mostly get blank stares.

BONUS STRATEGY

Now that you understand what steps you need to take to **NOT** be a victim anymore, I want to talk about the #1 Sin you should **never commit** when you're planning your various programs. It's very simple...Never, Ever, Ever be Boring! I'll say it again because it's worth repeating...you cannot ever, *ever* bore people.

Again, most of the time it isn't your fault. Most owners, or the people they delegate to handle their "advertising," become complacent in how they advertise and do the same thing over and over and over again. Or, worse yet, they follow the lousy examples set by the big chain restaurants (more on that a tad later).

What do I mean when I say "boring" advertising? You put an ad in the paper for 20% off. Snooze! Or putting an ad in the local coupon books (like ValPak) or the Entertainment Books just like what everybody else in there is doing. Snore! "Buy one get one free," "Get 20% off," "Get a free appetizer"...ZZzzzzzz. Those offers have been done repeatedly and the public has grown numb to them. Of course, it doesn't mean that some people won't redeem them, but generally it's folks who only eat at a restaurant when they find the "discount" in the paper.

As we discussed in the Holiday Marketing chapter, you can create an event or find an "excuse" to celebrate almost anything.

In addition to big "days" like Mother's Day, Father's Day etc:

Find a "day" to create a buzz around, or create one of your own. You can celebrate your anniversary, your dog's birthday, your business's anniversary, your grandpa and grandma's birthdays, anniversary, etc. Or honor somebody important in your life, perhaps somebody who is a positive example in your community.

One of the mistakes we all make (besides being BORING), is that we all have a tendency to want every guest we can get. Remember this statement (I have said it before, and I'm going to keep saying it all the way through this book)... Not All Guests Are Created Equal.

NOTE: When you're getting ready to do any marketing, one of your major strategies should be figuring out who is your *best guest*.

This will help you in figuring your demographics, which we talked about in an earlier chapter. Then ask yourself what is the best way to reach them? Another big mistake an independent restaurant owner can make is trying to copy what the big chains are doing. I see many restaurants, in today's market, trying to follow the big chains, but I'm here to tell you...it doesn't work!

It's important to understand that the chains operate by a different set of rules because their priorities are different from yours. What do chain restaurants really want? They want to focus on their *brand*, burning it, and churning it through guests with no desire to develop relationships or retention. And what do the big box chains have that you don't? They have a ton of money. They've got hundreds and thousands of chains all over that are all paying their "brand fees."

Subsequently, the corporate office can do multi-million dollars worth of generic advertising for them. For example, here in

Michigan there are 35 Chili's® restaurants. Corporate can afford to pay to put one Chili's ad on TV and run it throughout the state of Michigan, because everybody who sees it can "apply" it to their local chain, making it highly profitable. However, as an independent restaurant owner with one or two restaurants, the cost of putting an ad on the TV isn't feasible because you take too big of a hit with a massive, upside down ROI.

Here's an example of where great intentions and ambitions resulted in detrimental results. A friend of mine (name being withheld to protect the innocent) in Arizona has three up-scale restaurants. In order to keep up with the chains, he decided to do a mass media TV blitz and ended up spending over $150,000. Now, he had this sweet talking advertising rep selling him on the idea of making tons of money with "saturation marketing" (that was a big term coming from such a young kid!).

Well, my friend bought the idea hook, line and sinker and spent his $150,000. As you probably guessed it, his monthly receipts did increase, but only by $130,000 (so he immediately lost $20,000, plus the costs of all the extra staff he employed to help handle the oodles of extra business). Now, being a fairly smart marketer, he did get the new guests' names by having them sign up for his loyalty program. However, he also admitted that many of his existing guests came in from the ad, so he had no idea how many *new* clients he received from his TV media blitz. Oh, by the way, his offer was Buy One Get One Free...

Let me tell you a really great benefit about being an independent restaurant. You can react to the market quickly, change direction, and do things that big chain restaurants cannot.

NOTE: Take advantage of this type of adaptability...look for things in the news and utilize vendor specials to consistently increase your margins throughout your strategies.

For example, say that there's an overabundance of crab this week from your distributor and he gives you an offer on crab that you can't refuse. You can go out and advertise a "Crab Week" in the blink of an eye using your house list. A local family's home burns down...host a benefit dinner for them with part of the proceeds going to help with their needs. Big (and I'll add, Dumb) Chains plan their marketing ten months in advance and can't react as quickly as you can and change with current events.

Learn to manage your "house list" and become a real rainmaker in your community...becoming attentive to the needs of the local market. For example, if you're in Detroit, home of the Woodward Dream Cruise, you build an event around the Woodward Dream Cruise. If a particular sporting team is having an exceptionally good season, you can build around the whole winning theme. Even a team that is torturing their fans with an abysmally bad season (ever heard of the Detroit Lions?) can stimulate an event. There was one pizza restaurant in town willing to give a free pizza away when the Lions won their first game.

NOTE: Be Different...Be Exciting!!!

Whatever you do, keep it interesting, funny, and relevant... never boring. There are a lot of fun things you can do that the big chains wouldn't dare, other restaurants don't have the knowledge to do, or a "designated marketer" wouldn't have the concern, the ability, the desire, or the hunger to make these things work like an independent owner will.

In our new and emerging economy, it is now more important than ever to implement marketing strategies. Our objective is to make independent restaurants thrive and become important players of their communities and families. It is a crying shame when a good business has to close its doors. And these days, there is no neutrality…business is either going up, or it's crashing down. I am writing this book in 2010, and for the first time in my lifetime (60+ years), I have seen more independent restaurants go out of business than have come into the business. There is a real "thinning of the herd" process going on and those who are growing with their marketing are in a great position to really cash in.

As we say, money follows brains and ingenuity and you have to have consistent, out of the box strategies to get new customers through your door. Also, it is more important than ever that you retain your existing guests. If you go out haphazardly, marketing all over in every direction… "Oooh, I'm going to try Entertainment Book. Oooh, let's try radio. Hey, how about TV. Let's put a $10 certificate in the paper they can clip out! Oh, what I will do is, I won't take the time to get a guest list (because it's too much work), however, I will give everybody that comes through the door a 20% discount!"…then all you're really doing is kidding yourself and, before you know it, you may soon be out of business. In today's economy, you must have accurate thinking and measurable results!

NOTE: Know your numbers: both operationally and in marketing.

I'm going to reiterate a crucial point here…the number one strategy is: get your house list updated. You have to do that, and I'm going to harp on that. In fact, I'll be like your father…I am going to harp on you (in your head, like a monotone chant) to get your house list started and/or updated today! (Well, maybe I can be like your favorite uncle or someone). *However, you need to get your list today*. Remember, if you don't have a house list you only have acquaintances, not guests. A guest is somebody that you can invite over and over to come into your house any time you want. If you do not have their name, telephone, address, and their email they are acquaintances and can come and go any time they want to and will do so elsewhere.

ACTION PLAN

1. I will get my house list updated TODAY.

2. I will never let my marketing be boring and will rely on a diverse arsenal of strategies to market my restaurant. I will brutally and honestly measure all my marketing by knowing my numbers.

3. I will look for opportunities that are both local and national to tie in a promotion that helps both my restaurant and my neighbors.

4. I will never be an advertising victim again.

5. I will always measure my results.

CHAPTER 8
500,000,000 & Growing...
Facebook Marketing For Restaurants
by Urvi Mehta

What Are Facebook Pages?

A Facebook Page is the hub for your restaurant that lets you showcase your restaurant in front of millions of Facebook users in your local area. For independent restaurants it's the perfect outlet to the millions of users on Facebook (thousands in the local area) to know about their restaurant. Just like a Facebook personal profile, a restaurant can share photos, videos, information, articles, and special recipes of the week – all for free and without the hassle of learning any programming or HTML.

Facebook Pages are a great way for a business to have a visible and professional presence on Facebook. All Facebook users now have the ability to have a personal profile and create one or several Business Pages for their business, a cause, or anything they like and care about.

Why Most Restaurant Websites Fail

There are thousands of restaurants without a website. If you are one of them or your website was last updated five years ago, then know that this is really hurting your ability to be found by potential guests, as more and more individuals are doing searches online before they actually try a new restaurant. They want to read reviews (on Yelp, Facebook and other restaurant review websites), and do random searches (Google Maps) to see what comes up if they want to try a new restaurant. Quite simply, if you don't have any *visible* online presence, you're not going to be found by these guests. They are going to head over to your competition tonight.

If you have not gotten around to creating a great website because you cannot afford to hire a great web design company for couple of thousand dollars; well, don't worry - you can create a mini-website using Facebook's technology with literally a couple of clicks.

Let Your Guests Tell Their Friends About Your Restaurant

As guests came into your restaurant, let them know that now you have a Page on Facebook and ask them to become a fan of your Fan Page. It is free. It is easy. They are already used to doing it for things they care about. It only takes one click. When they become a Fan for your restaurant, an update gets sent to their Facebook friends that they have become a fan of your restaurant Fan Page. Now, all of their friends can find out about your restaurant and some of them will check you out. It is word of mouth marketing at its best.

Facebook Fan Pages are open and public. No one needs to ask permission from anybody to become a fan.

Let me give you an example. As I am writing this, I have about 3500 friends on Facebook. If I were to go out tonight and have dinner at a nice Italian restaurant and the service was pretty good, I liked everything, the ambience was great, and then I got home and looked the restaurant up or maybe they gave me a card with their Facebook Fan Page address on it. If I clicked LIKE on the Fan Page, 3500 of my friends will know within a matter of seconds that I LIKE this restaurant. They will know via a little update that pops up in their news feed, as Facebook calls it, updates, stating that I have become a fan of Angelo's Italian Restaurant. And if I were to post something on that restaurant fan page's wall; if I said, "Hey, we came in tonight, great experience, loved the food, loved the ambience," it takes it another step further and my friends would see that too.

The Price Of This Incredible Word Of Mouth Marketing

It is completely free for you to create a Fan Page. It's free to utilize all the popular applications that are already built into Facebook (photos, videos, reviews, events) that help you make your Page interesting and generate business. You can even automate to where you do not have to work on it everyday, sitting in front of a computer. And the only thing that Facebook charges for is Facebook ads.

Your investment is your time and the only time that you would need to pay for the Facebook Page is if you had a third party company create the Page for you. Let's say you don't have the time, even though it takes maybe 10 minutes to create a Page; there are still people that are unsure about going that step. You can hire other companies to create a Page for you. This is one of the services that my company PR Easy (www.PReasy.com/restaurants) provides for small independent restaurants and several other small businesses niches. We create and manage high quality Facebook Pages that people love visiting over and over again and refer their friends to. Our goal for your restaurant is to get you the right fans and keep your Page alive by updating your status and helping you share your content.

Is Your Website "Alive"?

One of my personal pet peeves is that most business websites get built and then they are left alone. It's not uncommon to go to a website and see that it was updated five years ago. You can actually see the date at the bottom of the web Page.

Hey, this is your business that you're putting out there in front of thousands of potential guests and if you're not actively putting in time to keep your customers and your future guests knowledgeable and engaged in what's going on and what's new with you, then how do you expect them to do business with you? How do you expect them to come back to you? You have to constantly be updating your network as to what you're doing, such as the new menu items you're launching. If you have new dishes and you have a new chef, new staff; maybe you have a new program that you've launched such as loyalty rewards, or maybe you have a recipe of the month. Either way, you want to let people in your area know all the new things you are doing so they come back to you over and over again.

Social media, social networking sites...I mean, the name tells you right there. You need to be networking with these folks out there. Facebook has more than 450 million registered users and half of that population is logging in every single day, and the average time that they spend is fifty-five minutes.

That is absolutely insane; almost an hour a day is being spent by 225 million people on Facebook. That number just increases. So, if you are not posting information out there for them to come back to you, ignoring it like a website, not updating it ever, then you are missing out on one of the easiest and fastest ways to promote your restaurant.

How Often You Should Update Your Facebook Page

My recommendation to my restaurant clients is to update their Page at least once a day, in the morning or in the afternoon. Make it something that you do on a daily basis and if you cannot do something on the weekend, then at least try to do it Monday through Friday. For our restaurant clients, especially when starting out, we recommend updating their Page seven days a week. Make it fun. Don't stress yourself on it. Take a daily picture of specials on the menu and give a brief description of the dish for the day or a short update like: *"Folks, we are going to have a beautiful day outside. Our patio is open, come and check it out."*

Facebook Page updates are short and quick. Facebook users do not like to read long updates. Keep them straight to the point and if you can share something once a day, it will really help keep your fans keep coming back to your Page and keep your restaurant name alive and well in their mind.

Get Their Attention On Their Cellphones

There are millions of people who choose to get their Facebook updates on their cell phone. The Facebook application is the most popular social networking app on the iPhone since the day it came out. Now imagine a full car of friends driving along, and I am the one in the backseat thinking of where to go and eat right now. Or maybe I am thinking about it as I am going to pick up my date or my spouse, dad, co-workers, and I see an update from your restaurant page pop up on my cell phone. It might be a picture, might be information about your special for tonight and I instantly make a decision to come to your restaurant. You just got a 4-topper.

Put Things On Facebook Pages That Will Interest Your Fans

On your Page, you can post other things such as healthy living tips or things to do around your community. Now keep in mind that the Facebook community likes to get free knowledge. They want to get as much information as they can without having to pay for it. Maybe there is something they can do in the area before or after visiting your restaurant. Maybe there is a movie theater close to your place. Talk about a nice park near your restaurant where they can walk around or maybe a coffee and dessert place near by that they can visit. Talk about sporting events that are happening around you.

A Fast Guide To Gaining Local And Right Fans

1. Reach out to your existing customer base, because they are going to be the first ones to join. I am talking about your database of guests that come regularly to your restaurant. You have gotten their permission to email them (read the chapter on Email Marketing). Send them an email and open with, *"Hey, we are just trying Facebook. We would love for you to become a fan of our Page. Just click here…"*

2. Ask your fans to suggest your Page to their friends. Do it by sending them a polite email asking for them to recommend your Page to their friends, as you are working on getting more fans to your Page. Tell them you really appreciate their help and support if they can suggest your Page to 5-10 friends on Facebook.

I help many businesses build and manage Facebook Pages. In my opinion, as long as they have a positive experience with your business, you will have their support in recommending your Page to other people.

3. When you give your guests the check for their meal, insert a card that says: *We are on Facebook. Please join us. We'd love to have you become a fan. We send out recommendations or a recipe of the month.* Give them a benefit. You can run a promotion or a contest where your guests submit their stories and experiences of coming into your restaurant with the best story getting a $20 gift certificate or 2 free glasses of wine on their next visit. Make it personal, let's say you are a high end Italian restaurant and someone proposed to their wife there, or they have an anniversary celebration or rehearsal dinner and they can share their experience and their stories on your Fan Page.

Again, when they're clicking over to your Page and sharing, their friends are going to see that they have shared on your Fan Page. So that'll help your Fan Page to be seen in their personal network of friends.

4. Host an event. If you are opening a new restaurant, announce your grand opening and build some buzz around it. You can actually use Facebook Events to create the event on Facebook itself and your fans would be notified that you have an event and then they can also share the event with their friends, and invite them also with just one click.

5. Run Facebook ads. Facebook ads are a great way for you to target your ideal customer. If you have been in business for awhile, you know who your ideal customers are: age, gender, occupation and likes/dislikes. Do you sell a lot of wine? How about targeting local wine lovers?

Facebook ads are powerful as they allow you to target *who* you're looking for versus what someone *could be* looking for.

POWER TIP: CONNECT FACEBOOK WITH TWITTER

Login to your Facebook account and then go to www.Facebook.com/twitter. With two clicks you can connect your Twitter account to your Facebook Page so anytime you update your Facebook Fan Page, it will also update your Twitter account. In this case, you will have the same message going to both networks without having to copy and paste it in both places.

The benefit of that is, let's say someone's connected to you on Twitter, but they're not connected with you on Facebook; once Facebook sends that update, they will shorten the update to 140 characters as with Twitter, you have the limitation of a hundred and forty characters. Facebook will only display a certain amount of characters and then there will be a link to take them back to the original post on your Facebook Page. If someone likes what you have sent out, and they're not fans with you on Facebook, if they click the link, it takes them to your Facebook Fan Page and now they have an option of becoming a fan of your restaurant as long as they have an account on Facebook.

Get A Personal Address For Your Restaurant On Facebook

A trend that is gaining steam every month: big brands and even movies that are advertising their upcoming releases or launches on TV are sending people to Facebook instead of to their websites. As a result, you'll see URLs like facebook.com/vitaminwater or facebook.com/EatPrayLoveMovie.

You need to get a customer URL for your Facebook Page as soon as possible.

It's a great way to brand your name with Facebook, because you can have a Facebook.com address for your restaurant which is easy to remember and print in your marketing instead of the long web address Facebook gives you when you create a Page.

You can do this in two easy steps:

1. Once you create the Fan Page for your restaurant, get 25 fans.

2 Log in to your Facebook account and go to www.Facebook.com/username and then select your custom username for your restaurant. You want to do this as soon as possible because if there is another restaurant out there that may have the same name but in a different city or different State, you want to make sure you grab it before they do. Keep in mind Facebook is used all around the world; again they have 450 million users so you do have to be quick here.

I do come across a lot of Facebook Pages who have hundreds, and in some cases, thousands of fans, and yet they don't have a vanity URL. Many businesses just don't know that a vanity URL exists or they don't know the benefits of how easy it can be to share their Fan Page with others if they were to just use their username. Big mistake.

Using Facebook Pages With Your Old Restaurant Website

You have a website that gets you lot of business. Great. Let's make it better.

Facebook allows the owners of its Pages to send traffic from their websites to Facebook and back. I made a simple video that you can see at TheFullRestaurantBook.com/ActionPlan. It is called a Fan Box. Once you've created the Page, Facebook will give you couple of lines of code that you can email to your webmaster and they will add that to your existing website. It will show up as a snapshot of your Fan Page and lists how many fans you have. If someone comes to visit your website, they can become a fan directly from your website with one click.

I strongly recommend that if you do have a website, create a Fan Page and add the Fan Box to your website. Most importantly display it in a position so that when someone comes to your website, they're going to see your Fan Box immediately. If you put it below the fold or you put it on one of the inner Pages, like on a "Contact Us" Page, or a "Learn More About Us" Page, not everyone will go to those Pages. So give it good real estate and position it right on your home Page where anybody that comes to your website will see it and act on it immediately. You will increase your fans right away.

What If Somebody Says Something Bad About Your Restaurant On Your Page?

If you have a negative comment and someone is just trying to bash your restaurant on Facebook, the best way to minimize the PR damage is to respond. If you leave it unattended or you delete it, it actually makes it look worse on your end. The best thing to do is to respond to their issues. Maybe it was they came in and they had a terrible experience with the food. Or they ordered something and it wasn't served that same way. Invite them to come back and experience the restaurant again, on you. Ask them to give it one more chance.

Or if you find that there is someone who is continuously posting negative comments for no reason, they could be one of your competitors or someone with nothing better to do with their time. If they're continuously posting negative comments, you can always remove someone from your Fan Page as well. You can block them permanently if they become a problem, and actually report them to Facebook.

Here is another way of looking at it, though. When I am reading a book review on Amazon and all the reviews are saying that this is the best book ever written, I don't know. My guard goes up. I wonder if the author actually asked all their cousins to write reviews on Amazon.

But if I see a review which says, "You know what, it's a good book. It didn't change my life and it's probably not for people like me. It's for a different crowd," it lends a certain level of authenticity to the overall book review.

Same also goes for reviews on Yelp and other restaurant review websites. It definitely makes it real. You don't want to only see positive reviews because then it does feel like it's fake and that it is just your family and staff members posting there. You definitely want to see the good and the bad because it gives you an overall experience of what a visit could be like or what your experience could be like based on other people's experiences.

I am not one for writing fake reviews. If it's a friend or even a family member, I don't want them to put fake reviews up. I'd actually want to go through the experience and then honestly put how that experience was. Instead of actually asking family members or even friends to go out there, I would go to Yelp and see who some of the strong local contributors on Yelp are. Who is someone that likes to go to new restaurants and test out the food and actually write real reviews?

I would connect with them on Yelp. See if they're on Facebook and even connect with them there. Invite them to come out to your restaurant and ask if they'd be willing to write a review on Yelp or on your Facebook Fan Page.

Love foodies in your zip codes. They are great because they will share their experience with other local foodies or friends and their social network, and they'll ask them to also go out and experience your restaurant and write reviews on your restaurant. Tap into that group before tapping into your friends and family members for fake reviews.

Emailing Your Facebook Page Fans Within Facebook

Facebook does not give you the ability to send emails but allows you to send updates to your Fans within Facebook. With this your fans will actually see the update in their InBox on Facebook under the update section. It's not a direct message. As people become more and more fans of Fan Pages, they get used to checking the update section.

Use this to promote an upcoming event, or a new dish that you might be trying out at your restaurant, or even to remind them to get their reservations in for Mother's Day or Valentine's Day. You can feature your chef or a different employee each week sharing a favorite dish.

I wouldn't recommend sending only updates on a daily basis because people on Facebook don't want to get messages all the time in their InBox from a business. For the daily updates you can do that on the Page itself. That is what the Page is for. When you're sending out an update as an email, do it maybe once a week and close to the weekend.

Updates would work great for any type of upcoming holiday. Mother's Day is great because people love to go out for a Sunday brunch or take their parents out for dinner. It doesn't always have to be a special. It can be, "Hey by the way, did you know that we also host? We have a banquet facility where we can host a graduation party or rehearsal dinner." "Or even that we have a new dessert that we've put on the menu. Come and taste the new dessert."

You can send an update on anything that is going on with the restaurant.

Using Photos To Promote Your Restaurant

Pictures are a great strategy to use for marketing on Facebook. More and more folks are putting pictures on Facebook. Facebook actually has over a billion photos uploaded each month, which is more than Flicker, a dedicated photo sharing site owned by Yahoo. People love sharing information on Facebook and they love responding to pictures. Pictures are one of the easiest ways to get your fans to comment. Show beautiful photos of your dishes, or the ambiance of your restaurant from the inside. Also, share photos of yourself and your chef.

Do not just make the Fan Page about the restaurant as a business. Add your personality. In order to make it more personable, you want to add those photos of the people that work for you. Even share photos of some of your regular customers that come in. People love to have their pictures put on Facebook.

You can tag them (think of tagging somebody as telling Facebook WHO this person is) and when you tag a person, their friends will also see an update saying that, *"Sally Morgan has been tagged in this photo by Angelo's Restaurant Page."*

Don't stress about taking professional pictures. You don't want to make the pictures look so professional that the people are afraid to upload pictures as they come. On Facebook, not only can you as the Page owner upload photos, but you can also let your fans upload photos. If you only have professional looking photos up, then your fans might not be comfortable posting something to your Fan Page off of their cell phone.

Have some professional photos but also have some fun photos that you take around the restaurant and make sure that you set your settings on your Fan Page to allow your fans to upload their own photos.

Using Short Videos On Your Restaurant Facebook Page

Videos are another great way to help local customers know more about you and your restaurant. Here are some video ideas that you can do yourself:

1. Take your video camera into the kitchen and tape a short, three minute video of the chef preparing one of the restaurant's favorites. Perhaps some of the favorites for which the restaurant is recognized – your signature dish.

2. Take a video of the interior of the restaurant. Is it more of an upscale setting or is it more of a lounge; what does the inside look like?

3. Get video testimonials of customers and upload those as well. Let's say a bridal party is going on with 10 guests and they've just told the waiters that they love the food, just ask them nicely, "Do you mind saying that in the camera for our Facebook Page?" Get their permission and put that up!

4. Invest in a video camera that you're going to keep at the restaurant; you don't want to forget it at home or forget it in a car. You can capture these moments as they're happening. For less then $100 you can get a great video camera at your local Best Buy or Amazon.com.

5. Educate your guests with fun things that everybody wants to know. Turn the camera on, put it on a tripod (you can buy that also from Amazon.com for around $20), sit down on the bar, just you, nothing fancy, then talk about something completely unscripted on something that interests people. Here are some ideas:

- The difference between ordering dried pasta versus fresh pasta

- If you're ordering veal, what kind of wine you should be ordering with veal and why

- Tell the story of one of your dishes. Where does it come from?

The restaurant owners have such a great opportunity for talking about food. They don't even have to think about ideas for videos. They probably have 200-300 videos already in their head.

- If I am ordering the restaurant's signature dish, does white wine go better or is it going to be red? And which red, is it a Merlot or a Cabernet?

Give tips like that and when you upload these videos on Facebook, you can also upload them to YouTube. With this, you have more viral marketing coming back to your restaurant at no cost to you.

If you don't have your own website, when you upload a video into YouTube, you can put the link to your Facebook Page, so when people are looking on YouTube and they see your video, they can link back to your Facebook Page as well.

Facebook Advertising To Attract Even More Fans

My company (www.PReasy.com/restaurants) creates and manages ad campaigns on Facebook for many types of small business owners and without a doubt, it is one of the smartest and most cost effective advertising in which a small restaurant can invest.

To continue with our example of an Italian restaurant owner, your customers are mostly couples, living within 5 miles of the restaurant, average age over 30, and visiting with a date or significant other. You get lots of couples and everybody likes to drink wine.

How can you use Facebook ads to get more of these guests to come into your restaurant?

Facebook knows a lot about its users because when someone creates an account, they're giving a lot of information, not really knowing that they're giving out a lot of information to complete their profile. Their age, gender, relationship status, the city they are located in, their likes – everything goes in their Facebook Profile. People love to share information about their likes, their dislikes, what it is that they're doing, the type of food that they like to eat, the type of things that they like to drink, the type of movies they like and so on.

You can zero into each of these things and find your target customer, your target prospect. Let's say there's a large corporation around you. For example: we have a restaurant in Dearborn, Michigan. The Ford Motor Company is really big in Dearborn. That's where their headquarters is located. We can search for folks that have indicated that they work at Ford Motor Company that live in the metro Detroit area. We can target ads to them with lunch specials to bring them in during the lunch hour.

Local Targeting

Most restaurants, I would say, typically get business from a local customer base. Maybe five miles, maybe ten miles. Facebook lets you target people who live close to your restaurant. You can input the city where your restaurant is located, and then it allows you to zero in on that location based on 10 miles, 25 miles and 50 miles. You can just put in 10 miles within your city name. And what Facebook is really good at doing, is that as you are putting in these parameters, it will tell you how many individuals your ad would be displayed to. So based on the parameters I've put in, it is going to reach 5,000 potential folks or maybe 50,000. You can gear your budget according to that number as well.

Making A Facebook Ad Budget That Works For You

There are two ways that you pay for the Facebook ads. You can do it for *cost per click*, where whenever anyone clicks on the ad, you're going to pay a certain amount, or you can do a *cost per impression* where you pay per 1,000 times your ad is shown to Facebook users who live locally. The minimum Facebook asks you to spend is $1 per day. And if you are setting up your ads correctly, even a $5 per day budget can get you incredible results.

The great thing about Facebook is that you can adjust your ads on the fly. Start a campaign, let it run for two or three weeks and see what kind of response you're getting, and then you can make an adjustment based on the feedback from Facebook Insights, which is a great tool that Facebook provides for free to its Page owners.

The biggest tip I can give you if you are planning to run your own ads on Facebook is this: make sure that the ad has a compelling headline. You also want to include a photo with the ad. As a restaurant owner, I would get a photo of one of your tastiest dishes. Something to start with could be a dessert or a glass of wine with one of your dishes to compel the person to look at the ad.

ACTION PLAN

1. Create the Page with your restaurant name in the title. Keep in mind that when you create the Page, Facebook does not allow you to change the title, so be sure everything is spelled correctly.

2. Add contact numbers, put in your information, add a few photos and some videos. Get a couple of posts on there on the wall for your Fan Page because people don't want to come to an empty Page. Get that going, and then start on the next step. Just take that first step. Keep in mind, if you make a mistake or if you post something that you don't like, you can always delete it.

3. After you've added a few things, get to your 25 fans as fast as possible so you can secure the URL, the user name for

your Fan Page. After you've got the 25, start engaging with your fans that are on there. Ask your existing guests, your own friends on Facebook to "Fan you up" so you can get to 25 fans within a day or so. Send me an email at urvi@preasy.com and I will fan you up also.

4. Ask your fans to share some stories. Ask them some questions. Post some more information. Get them to suggest the Fan Page to their friends and start building more fans as you're going along.

5. Customize by adding in some applications. If you do a lot of videos and you don't want to upload them directly to Facebook, and you do have them already on YouTube, you can add a YouTube application to where it will upload into your Facebook Fan Page.

6. You also want to create a custom landing Page. What I mean by this is you can use an application on Facebook called Static FBML. It stands for Facebook Markup Language, which just means Facebook HTML. You can paste this as a welcome tab, where anyone who is not a fan can actually come to your Fan Page and land on this Page.

7. Start running Facebook Ads. Get your first campaign going. You don't want to spend a lot of money. You can start with as little as $50 to $100 a month to start.

8. Start getting reviews from your customers by giving them little cards that say, "Hey, we're on Facebook. Come and join us on Facebook and share what you like about us." Facebook has a reviews tab that you can add when you're ready to start getting feedback from your fans. Go ahead

and add that tab and your customers can write reviews right there for you.

Urvi Mehta is a passionate Social Media Evangelist who thrives on teaching and consulting business owners and organizations on how to effectively use Web 2.0, social media marketing tools and social networks like Facebook, Twitter and LinkedIn to create buzz, traffic and profits while increasing their branding online.

Urvi Mehta is a co-founder of PR Easy. PR Easy is a client focused full service internet marketing company which serves clients in US, Canada, UK and Australia. At PR Easy we provide Training, Consulting and various Done-4-You services which radically increases client's presence online which gets them massive exposure and web traffic to their website. PR Easy focuses on creating marketing campaigns which results into very qualified prospects for their clients thus increasing client's bottom line. PR Easy provides Search Engine Marketing, Search Engine Optimization, Social Media Marketing and Landing Page Creation services to business owners.

BONUS

Discover how Restaurant Owners are using Facebook fan pages right now to bring more patrons to their business and create raving fans that come back over and over again.

Click on the link below to download A FREE Training Video On
"5 Key Elements Restaurant Owners Should Have On Their Facebook Fan Page"

Visit http://www.PReasy.com/restaurantmarketing

CHAPTER 9
Twitter Marketing for Restaurants
by Mark Ijlal

A Taco Truck Becomes A Smash Success

Caroline Shin-Manguera and Chef Roy Choi had a crazy idea one late night. Use a taco truck to sell Korean BBQ tacos in Los Angeles.

This would not be the first taco truck to have a long and tasteful history of making hot fresh tacos for hordes of hungry lunch goers and late night club goers. But it would be the first delivering Korean BBQ tacos – something that nobody had ever heard of before in LA.

As the founders tell the story...the initial days were hard. Some days they made few sales. Some days they ended up eating most of their tacos before they went bad. In some rough areas of LA, the local street gangs screamed at them for turning a Latino dish into something nobody had ever heard of before.

Somebody told the founders about Twitter one day. Twitter had been around for almost two years at that time and it seemed that everybody in the media world, from CNN anchors to Jim Carrey to Oprah, could not stop raving about the 140 characters or less messaging service. Ashton Kutcher challenged CNN and won to become the first person that was being followed on Twitter by one million people. Oprah joined and then broadcasted LIVE in all caps. But then again, if you are Oprah, you can do whatever you want. Caps or no caps.

Twitter was hot. And it was free to join and use. In short, a taco truck/restaurant operation like Kogi BBQ which was struggling to keep their truck running on the streets of LA, had absolutely nothing to lose for joining and using a free service.

So Kogi BBQ joined Twitter (twitter.com/kogibbq) and started telling those few people who were brave enough to try their Korean BBQ tacos that they could find out where the taco truck was going to be the next day and at what time if they just checked them out on Twitter and followed Kogi BBQ – *follow* is Twitter speak for your permission to somebody – a person or a business – to send you short 140 character messages to your cell phone or via web.

Well, the tacos were pretty good. Actually most people said that these were the best tacos that they ever had and they wanted to eat them again. So people started following them on Twitter.

Kogi BBQ, desperate to make any sales to keep their business going, kept announcing their truck schedule – "(EspeciaL:TurkeyTortaTango(griLLed turkey, kimchi, cheese, refried "beans on soft angel breastesses known as SaLvadorian piLLow buns),$7" and their incoming truck location: <u>630PM-9PM@Irvine Office & Storage (8 Whatney.); 1030PM-12AM@Concourse Entertainment Center (3364 E. La Palma Ave. Anaheim)</u> They also included where the truck is going to be in the next 30 minutes via their cell phones as they were traveling.

As people were eating these tacos, some of them were announcing to their friends about the "best taco I ever ate at Kogi BBQ truck." So their friends came the next day to check out the Kogi BBQ truck and when they liked the tacos, they went back on Twitter and said the same thing.

The word had started to spread.

From 10 followers on Twitter to 100, then to 500, 1000, 5000 and it kept spreading. The truck started selling out. They added one more truck. Those days of praying for just selling enough to keep the truck going were over. Now there were mobs of people who were checking out Kogi BBQ on Twitter to make sure that they wouldn't miss the truck.

As Kogi BBQ buzz grew, the reporters who were already in love with Twitter kept hearing about this taco truck. Soon stories about Kogi BBQ started appearing in newspapers and on TV reports.

Kogi BBQ, within 12 months, had gone from an obscure taco truck barely surviving to make gas money, to a huge brand with four trucks. As I write this, Kogi BBQ's Twitter "followers" exceed 74,000 and the number is growing every day. They have four taco trucks now aptly named Azul, Verde, Naranja, and Roja and even a physical location called The Alibi Room.

Kogi's story is unique and you may not have a taco truck, but you can still use Twitter to drive more business to your restaurant every night.

What Is Twitter?

Twitter is a social networking and micro blogging service that enables its users to send and read messages known as *"tweets."*

"Tweets" are text-based posts of up to 140 characters displayed on a personal or your restaurant's profile page and delivered almost instantly to the people who have given you permission to send updates about you or your business. Twitter calls these people

"followers."

Now you as a sender can get a couple of options on who can see your updates. If you have a personal account just for family use, then you can restrict delivery just to those in your circle of friends. By default, Twitter allows open access, meaning anybody can see your updates and become your restaurant's *follower*. All users can send and receive *tweets* via the Twitter website, text messaging or dozens of free software available for use with your phones or desktop computer. Twitter is free although if you choose to receive updates via text messaging, you might incur text messaging charges depending upon your cell phone plan.

Setup Your Twitter Account In 5 Minutes

1. Type www.Twitter.com in your web browser.

2. Click on "New To Twitter?"

3. Enter your first and last name.

4. Twitter will ask you to pick up a user name. Enter your restaurant name. Try to keep it short. Long names are tedious and easily misspelled. If your restaurant name is Angelo's Italian Restaurant, you should choose from these choices: Angelo's, AngelosItalian, or AngelosRestaurant. I don't recommend AngelosItalianRestaurant as it is way too long. Ideally you want as short a name as possible because your Twitter address will be www.Twitter.com/username so keeping it simple and short looks pleasing to eyes and is easy to spell.

5. Pick a password.

6. Enter your email address and check the box that says "Let others find me by my email address." Choose this especially if you have an email list and you are already sending promotional emails or newsletters to your existing guests list. This will insure if any of them join Twitter, they will be able to find you automatically, as Twitter has the ability to connect with existing email addresses and automatically display them so you can also follow your friends already on Twitter.

7. Click on "Create My Account."

8. Click on Settings and then on Profile. Add a picture of either yourself, a great picture of your dish or your restaurant logo.

9. Add location (Metro Detroit, Michigan), Website link if you have a website already or if you are using a Facebook Page instead of a website, link to your Facebook Page.

10. Add a short bio about your restaurant. Keep it simple. Kogi BBQ's bio simply says, "Korean BBQ Taco Truck." Yours could be "Family owned Italian Restaurant with famous Chicken Marsala Sauce."

11. Click on "DESIGN" and here you can select from pre-designed Twitter themes to give your restaurant Twitter page some color and personality. If you have a logo that you want to use as your background, you can even upload that here and see how it looks.

12. Click on "ACCOUNT" tab and scroll to "TWEET LOCATION." This is a powerful tool for local restaurants. When you checkmark this option, Twitter will include

location information like neighborhood, town, or exact point when you tweet. So when the 100 million and growing population of Twitter is looking for local restaurants to visit tonight, they will find you more easily.

13. You are almost done here but before you leave Twitter... what is your daily special tonight? Any drink specials going on? Test your new Twitter powers by clicking on "Home" and then sending 1 or 2 short updates about your menu for the night.

I also created a short five minute training video to walk you through everything I just taught you. Head over to TheFullRestaurantBook/ActionPlan and click on "Setup Your Twitter Account Video."

O.K. I Am On Twitter...Now What Do I Do?

The reason why you, my very busy restaurant owner, have joined Twitter is to create some buzz about your restaurant. To get people talking about you online and use Twitter as a great tool to get positive word of mouth and fill up your restaurant, night after night.

You don't want just a lot of people following you on Twitter. You want the *right people* following you on Twitter.

Twitter is free, but you will be investing some time in it to make it work for your restaurant. Just like a Facebook Page, a lot of restaurants are joining Twitter without a clue on how to use it to generate business. They join Twitter because they heard about it on TV or read an article about it online. After five days, they abandon Twitter in disgust and move on to something else.

Both Twitter and Facebook are littered with dead ghost town accounts that restaurant owners of all stripes started but never used to get any business.

We are not going to let you go that route.

But before you start, put some short updates about your restaurant on Twitter.

Here are five action steps to insure that you get the maximum bang on the time that you are going to invest to make Twitter work for your restaurant:

Step 1: Ask every guest in your restaurant every night to follow you on Twitter.

The best people to start with building a Twitter following are the folks who are already sitting in your restaurant and enjoying the food every night. Ask them nicely if they use Twitter and if they say YES, then ask them to follow you.

Make a little business card with your Twitter address. If you have already set up a Facebook Page, add that address also and tell your servers to give that card out to every guest who is a Twitter user so they won't forget.

Here are two benefits to teach your servers so they can tell the guests every night:

1. "Check us out on Twitter and make sure to follow us because we intend to do all sorts of special promotions like wine & beer tastings just for our Twitter family."

2. "Check us out on Twitter and make sure to follow us so whenever you come here again, you will know about our daily dinner and drink specials."

Step 2: Follow Foodies on Twitter.

I scratch my head when I see a restaurant following nobody. The beauty of Twitter is connecting to people who might find what you do very interesting. "Foodies" or people who love food, especially restaurant food, are a new tribe in the United States. The Internet and tools like Facebook and Twitter have given foodies enormous power to spread the word about your restaurant and its food almost instantly to their own fellow foodies and to people who keep track of what local restaurant they are currently raving about to make their own restaurant picks.

I want you to build a list of foodies in your city and metro area and have your restaurant Twitter account start following them.

Almost everybody on Twitter, besides the celebrities, always check back to see the new people who are following them. Think of it as meeting somebody at a cocktail party who politely asks you what you do for a living. After you have answered the question, what do you ask? Same question right? So when you follow somebody who has no idea who you are, they will check you out and most likely follow you out of a mix of curiosity and courtesy. The only time it does not happen is when you have a dead Twitter account.

1. Login to your Twitter account. On the top right hand side, click on "FIND PEOPLE" then type in your city's name and one by one, the following keywords: *foodie, food network, eating out, Top Chef, gourmet cooking, wine.* You can also add the type of cuisine

that you serve. For example an Italian restaurant can try searching for people on Twitter who like Italian food, Italian Cuisine, Love Pasta, etc. Once you discover people in your local area click "FOLLOW" to start following their updates on Twitter.

2. Another tool I really like to discover people who have interest in what I do is called Tweepz.com, that lets you limit searches to specific parts of Twitter's user information like name, bio, and location. So go to www.Tweepz.com and type in bio: "foodie loc: Detroit" (or whatever metro area you are in). Just by doing that, I found 21 foodies in the metro Detroit area. Repeat the search with the other keywords such as: *food network, eating out, Top Chef, gourmet cooking, and wine.*

3. If you already have a Facebook Page, ask people to follow you on Twitter. You might be thinking they are already checking you out on Facebook, why should you bother them to follow you on Twitter? Because the majority of Twitter users choose to get their Twitter updates on their cell phones. With Facebook you have to be logged in to get those updates. Let's say I am thinking about going out tonight with my friends. I just left work and I am calling four of my friends, one by one, trying to figure out where we should go for dinner.

As I am stopped somewhere, I get a text message from your Twitter account letting me know that all drinks are half off before 6pm. Bingo. You just made my decision for me. I call all my friends and we start heading toward your place. Although you are going to put this update on Facebook, (I will show you in a minute how Facebook and Twitter work together so you don't have to do double the work), I could not have received this update on your Facebook Page unless I logged into Facebook.

4. Do special things for your Twitter followers: A wine glass. A free appetizer. A complimentary dessert. Restaurant owners know how to make their regulars feel special. So do the same thing for your new Twitter family. If you want word of mouth marketing then you have to give people good reasons to talk about you on Twitter.

The more you make your Twitter followers *feel special* the more likely they are to go back and talk about you to their friends, who will talk about you to their friends and the circle gets bigger and bigger.

We all want to feel special. Yet most restaurants never had this kind of word of mouth opportunity before. Email is fine but email is still private. It goes from one person to another person and does not get opened up immediately. Very few people on your email list are likely to get up in the morning and happily start forwarding your promotions to everybody on their email list. Yet on Twitter, when people find something they like – they talk about it to everybody they know on Twitter. The word of mouth about your restaurant spreads and spreads.

So what kind of special promotions can you do for your Twitter followers? Here are some ideas to get you started:

- Host a wine tasting at your restaurant. Or a beer tasting. Announce it on Twitter. Ask people to invite their friends. Make sure to clarify that this is just a promotion for your Twitter friends.

- Teach something fun. How about hosting a fun class and teach people something that they don't know but they always wanted to know: The difference between dry and fresh pasta; what wine to order with which food; how to make restaurant quality soup at home very quickly. Put it out on Twitter. Ask them to come learn and bring their friends.

- Do a cooking class on a slow day or on a day that you are closed. Charge a small fee. There is a small high end Italian restaurant near my home. They charge a small fee to teach people how to make a three course dinner in their kitchen, then everybody sits down and eats what they just made. People who do it cannot stop talking about it. The restaurant is packed every night and gets great buzz.

5. Listen and respond to questions.

Twitter is not a text messaging service. SMS text messaging is another great tool to have in your toolbox, but Twitter is really a cocktail party conversation. As your Twitter family grows, you will be asked questions. People will ask you about your specials, about your promotions. Sometimes you might even get a 'complaint' about the service they received or not being able to get a reservation.

Sometimes you will be swamped with your work and we all know that running a restaurant is lots and lots of work. You will think, I don't have time today to respond to these questions; maybe I will do it tomorrow.

Don't.

Find a second and respond. It is sad but we have come to a point where people don't expect any kind of response from a business anymore. I am shocked if I call an 800 number and a human being answers on the other end instead of computer. When somebody asks you a question on Twitter and you respond fast – it is a pleasant surprise for them. Next time somebody in their own Twitter circle asks everybody to recommend a local restaurant, they are more likely to remember and recommend your restaurant because of your food, service, and ambience, but also because you showed that you cared by listening and responding.

The Secret Sauce: Add 'Personality' To Your Twitter Account

You have two choices on how you can use Twitter to promote your restaurant. The first is to use it to announce specials, promotions, and events: place your restaurant in front of people who might talk about it back to their own Twitter followers. Foodies and local food reporters are two examples. Kogi BBQ does all the above and is reaping huge rewards in buzz and sales from it. You can also add a little personality to your Twitter account by making your restaurant Twitter page stand out from every other restaurant. Here are some ways:

Add pictures. Free services like www.TwitcPic.com let you share pictures on Twitter. No need to go and take a professional photography course. Restaurant kitchens have bright fluorescents lights as it is. Take a picture of the dish before it goes out with your cell phone and upload it to Twitter.

- It is okay to share something funny about your business on Twitter. Most people find the restaurant business fascinating. I am not kidding. Take a look at all the food shows about restaurants on TV. If your fish vendor screwed up and delivered tilapia instead of halibut and you are standing in the kitchen trying to figure out how to switch your special tonight, share that thought on Twitter…It is much more interesting than a Twitter update about somebody about to walk into a boring meeting.

- Ask people's opinions. Let's say you are thinking about introducing two new dishes. Describe them and ask people to tell you which one makes them hungry.

- Thank people for following your restaurant on Twitter. A thank you is still the most powerful gift that a business owner can give to its customers. Sadly most businesses never do. Don't be one of them.

- Take pictures with your staff. Take pictures of your kitchen. Put them up. Let people see the human faces behind your restaurant.

Show Up Everyday

Your restaurant is open five or six days a week. Your marketing needs to be on seven days a week. The biggest mistake most restaurant owners make in their online marketing has nothing to do with ignorance. Meaning, if you chose not to setup a Facebook Page or setup a Twitter account or collect cell phone numbers from your guests because you had no idea until you began reading this book…that is fine.

But to setup a Facebook Page or a Twitter account, update it for a few days grudgingly and then only update it once every 10 days is the biggest mistake you can make in your online marketing.

Listen, everybody is busy. Everybody gets the same 24 hours that you and I get. But the most successful people in any business are good at prioritizing what is important and what will bring new business to them.

You don't need 15 minutes. You need 3 minutes or less to make your restaurant show up every day on my computer and my cell phone. Take a picture with your cell phone and post it on Twitter, using your cell phone keyboard to update your Twitter account for your restaurant. Almost all phones right now are coming pre-loaded either with small software programs called applications that let you use Twitter on your cell phone, or you can just text your updates to your Twitter account. Just send your "tweets" to **40404**. Simple as that.

Instead of being grumpy about it, add Twitter to your daily routine. Don't fight it. Don't argue with me. Just do it for 90 days straight. At best you are looking at 3 minutes of your time every day invested in it. Try it for 90 days. You will be surprised at the results.

Can you imagine where Kogi BBQ would be right now if there was no Twitter?

Some quick tips to build your followers and actually enjoy doing it:

- Make it fun. Count your Twitter followers. Make a goal to hit 100, 250, 500, 1000 followers.

- Run a contest between your followers. Tell them to put the word out about your restaurant to their friends on Twitter and when you hit 1000 followers, you will throw a wine tasting or do some kind of great promotion just for your Twitter followers.

- Do it everyday. Really. The same way you open up your restaurant everyday in the morning and turn on the lights. Update your Twitter account with the same regularity.

- Announce everything that would interest your customers and Twitter followers: daily specials, new appetizers, new seasonal dishes. "Hey, just got first batch of fresh asparagus for the season. Thinking of making it into a soup and side with steak." Also announce new additions to your wine list or cocktail drinks menu.

Link Up Facebook And Twitter

As Urvi Mehta brilliantly explained in her Facebook Page chapter, your restaurant can use a Facebook Page to be in front of millions of people who use Facebook every single day in your area. Facebook actually allows you to link up your Twitter account to your Facebook Page for your restaurant so every time you update your Facebook Page – your Twitter account will be updated automatically. Less work…double the effect.

Here are the quick steps to do it:

- Login to your Facebook account.

- Go to www.Facebook.com/Twitter

- Facebook will ask your Twitter username and password and within 2-3 clicks your Facebook Page will be linked to your Twitter account.

Go NAKED (Pizza)

Naked Pizza makes and sells pizzas in New Orleans. TechCrunch is the biggest tech blog in the world, based out of Silicon Valley. NY Times is a national newspaper published out of New York.

We will come back to these three in a minute.

Let me ask you a question…what is the most important business thing that is prominently displayed everywhere in a pizza shop? And I mean everywhere…on their signs, on their ads, on their coupons, everywhere?

If you said their phone number, you got it right. Pick up any ad from any pizza shop whether it's a chain, one location local or a gourmet shop selling $25 pies, and their phone number is everywhere because pizza is a phone number business. People have to call you to order their pizza ahead of showing up.

This pizza + phone number relationship has not changed in the last 50 or so years. So when Naked Pizza decided to skip the phone number route and instead erect a giant billboard with their Twitter address www.Twitter.com/NAKEDPizza, they got a little attention from the world outside New Orleans.

Think TechCrunch and NY Times type of headlines. Think Mark Cuban, owner of the Dallas Mavericks investing in the business to help the owners grow their business to a national level.

Nine thousand followers strong, NAKEDPizza has everything that a restaurant can do on its Twitter account. They make it fun. They talk about their daily specials. They explain their healthy menu choices. They ask for people to recommend them to their friends. And it keeps on growing. Follow them on Twitter to get your own daily inspiration on what you can and should be doing with your own restaurant on Twitter.

ACTION PLAN

1. Before you do anything watch the short five minute video TheFullRestaurantBook/ActionPlan on how to setup your Twitter account.

2. Head over to Twitter and create an account for your restaurant.

3. Upload a picture. Don't do anything until you have done that. A Twitter account without a picture is a dead account.

4. Write a short bio describing your restaurant – 2-3 lines are fine. You can always change it later.

5. Turn on the location feature.

6. Post some quick updates about your restaurant.

7. Find 20 foodies in your city and metro area to follow by logging in to your Twitter account and going to Tweepz.com Follow them.

8. Follow NakedPizza and even Kogi BBQ on Twitter.

9. Talk to your servers and start asking guests in your restaurant to start following you on Twitter.

10. Staple your Facebook / Twitter card to every check. I have two great templates for you to download and make your own at TheFullRestaurantBook/ActionPlan.

11. Update your Twitter account every day.

CHAPTER 10
Email Marketing For Restaurants
by Mark Ijlal

All smart restaurants collect email addresses from their guests so they can email updates and promotions. Make these small changes in your email marketing to get more guests showing up every night at your restaurant.

A. Don't make it all about coupons.

I have a word for it: **Coupon Fatigue**. *"Yes, but, but, but Mark..."* you sputter, *"everybody knows that people love restaurant coupons."*

Yes, they do. But imagine how your kids would feel if everyday was Christmas? If everyday when they came downstairs to get ready for school, there were a bunch of gifts underneath the Christmas tree? Pretty soon the excitement of Christmas Eve would turn into boredom. Your birthday is so magical because it is not every day. When all you do is push email coupons to your email list, after your email list already knows what is inside the wrapper...they really don't pay attention. Instead, they say to themselves, "There is nothing exciting in it beside a coupon and I am not going out tonight. I will just save this email and check it out when I am planning to go out."

The email is never opened. It stays in their Inbox and soon it is buried underneath another fifty other emails.

How many emails do you have right now in your Inbox that you have never opened?

Have you scheduled a time later this week to sit down, lock the door, and read every email one by one? Yeah, right!

Look, email has been around in its present form for fifteen years now. Nobody is excited JUST BECAUSE THEY GOT AN EMAIL. That was back in 1995. Now, billions of emails later, nobody feels obligated to open up your email and read it just because you typed up a bunch of lines and hit SEND.

It is inside the guts of the email, where now the battle is being fought to make your customers excited about getting something from you. There are two ways to win the hearts and clicks of your email list so they will open and respond to your emails. The first has to do with the *look* of your email and the second one has to do with what is *inside* your email.

Let's start with *looks and appearance.*

B. Make your email attractive.

The restaurant business to you and I is about running a business, food orders, busy nights, managing chefs and employees, and keeping your head above water in a recession, or competing head on with a rush of new restaurants (chain or independent) that inevitably open during good times.

A restaurant owner is busy running a business. But to the guests, a restaurant business is about the good and beautiful things in life: food, wine, drink, friends, family, good times, pretty dishes, and people in crisp uniforms.

When you are sending out an email that does not reflect all the above to your guests, you are flat out turning them off. Luckily what used to cost hours to do: create a beautiful looking email for a

126

restaurant, along with some mad skills in HTML and Photoshop, now takes less than 20 minutes using services like Constant Contact, which lets restaurant owners whip up professional looking emails in a matter of minutes and costs less than $20 per month. Go to http://TheFullRestaurantBook.com/ConstantContact for a detailed tutorial and more tips.

C. FREE does not equal CRAP.

Every time I open emails, a good 75% of them make me wonder if the senders of these emails would have sent me this crap if they were paying $100 for the privilege of emailing every person on their email list.

Just because email is free, or almost free, in most cases, it does not mean that it has to be crap. Here are five ways to avoid that harsh fate and make the guests on your email list look forward to getting your emails:

1. **Teach Them**: How about teaching them how to keep their lettuce fresh for three days, or the shortcut to making a killer gourmet cheese sandwich which their children will love?

2. **Dazzle Them**: You have knowledge about food and wine. Share the knowledge. You can talk about food and wine pairings, the difference between wheat and ale beers, or the mistakes people make to ruin a good steak or a roasted chicken.

3. **Make Them An Insider:** Instead of telling them about a new dish that you just added or the three new wines that you are adding to your wine special for next month, write

about why you chose the ones you did and why you rejected the ones you didn't choose.

4. **Be That Local Guy:** Restaurant business is local business. When you are driving to your restaurant in the afternoon and listening to the traffic and local news on your radio, so are your customers. I live in Detroit and only months ago, everybody living here took a big collective gulp when General Motors almost went under before declaring bankruptcy and reinventing itself as a more agile company. During those three tense months, every restaurant in the metro Detroit area had customers who worked for GM or one of its suppliers holding their collective breaths about the future of their jobs. A local restaurant could have run a "GM Employees, Forget The Stress" for one night, and given drink promos or some other special to the GM employees on its email list with a request for guests to forward the email to any other GM employees they knew. All they needed to get invited to the party was to show their GM employee identity card at the entrance. Imagine the goodwill a restaurant would create in their local community, with perhaps local press, providing a great night for patrons who were attending because everybody knew that they were in the same boat.

5. **Entertain Them:** I know that not everybody is a natural comic but every restaurant owner I know can entertain for hours with the funny stories they have accumulated over the years. Folks, you are in a business that is never dull or boring. Every day you are dealing with people and people are interesting. Try it. Share a funny story that you have been telling all your employees for years. Try telling it to your customers next. Make sure it is not off color or

offensive but hey, if you want to tell the story of the guy who came in on a first date and drank two bottles of wine in the first 30 minutes...I say go for it.

D. Where Are They Reading Your Email?

Do you know that probably a good 30% of your email list is reading your email on their mobile phone? And no, I am not talking about iPhone or Blackberry...every phone is a smart phone nowadays, even the ones that the cell phone carriers are giving away for free or for almost nothing. The increasing number of people texting and reading emails on their cell phones is only going to grow.

Ask your kids. Ask your servers. Ask your friends if they ever read their emails on their cell phones. If your guests are over 26 and under 40, take my word for it; they are reading some emails on their cell phones everyday.

That is why you want to vary the length of your emails. If you make all your emails like a newsletter, you will miss out on these folks. Make some emails short. Send a newsletter out once a month. But keep the connection going. If you are informing me about wine that your wine rep just brought you, that blew your head off because it is so good, and he is desperate to unload his entire 20 cases at a rock bottom price, tell your email list this whole story in five lines or less. Four paragraphs are not needed here.

E. Be Like TV.

One of the biggest mistakes everybody makes and yeah, I have done it too, although it was a long time ago, is to send emails out without a set schedule.

Think TV programming – they have a schedule. The daytime soaps come everyday at a certain time. Letterman and Leno come on at night at a certain time. The crime dramas start at a certain time. Every single week. Peace, wars, floods, storms, or sunshine – the TV schedule is like USPS; it is sacred to the people who manage it.

You should treat your email schedule like this too. If you say your email newsletter will be once a month, well, it better be a set day every single month that your email newsletter flies out. If you are planning to send short updates to your email list once a week on Thursday to remind them to drop by your restaurant on the weekend, well, that email better be written before Wednesday ends, and first thing Thursday morning you should be logging into your Constant Contact account and hitting SEND.

Two things happen here when you become serious about your email schedule. First, it makes you serious about email marketing. You will start looking at every opportunity to turn an aspect of your business into a short email or newsletter content to be shipped out when the day comes.

Second, it makes your customers serious since they are getting the drip, drip, drip instead of that, "Hey, I have not talked to you for six months because I have been busy, but here is a coupon" that goes for most restaurant email marketing nowadays.

HOW TO BUILD AN EMAIL LIST

One door is not enough.

I know what you are thinking…I already set up a Facebook Page and a Twitter account, thanks to Urvi and you hounding me about it. Now you are telling me I need to build an email list…am I not annoying my guests by so much contact?

No. No. No.

In the early days of the Internet, one door was more than enough. If you built an email list, you had a great asset. But the Internet is a teenager now, and like all teenagers, its attention is scattered all over the place.

You need to build an email list because not everybody will pay attention to you on Twitter or Facebook. Some will love your Facebook Page. Some will like your Twitter updates and some will like getting a great looking newsletter from you once a month plus occasional short updates that you will be sending them.

Start With What You Have

I have thousands of people on my email lists. There was a day when I just had one person.

It does not matter what you have right now. If you have never even thought about building an email list or sending newsletters, it doesn't matter. The past is past and it is worthless. Today is all that matters. Starting to build an email list today is what matters most.

Remember the card template I asked you to download and get 1000 copies made from our website: TheFullRestaurantBook/ActionPlan – there is another card template there for you to start building an email list from the best, most receptive audience any business owner can wish for…*the folks dining at your restaurant today.*

Here is what I want you to do:

1. Download the card template from TheFullRestaurantBook/ActionPlan.

2. Get at least 500 copies made. If you print 1000, you will probably get it done cheaper. There are links on our websites to several affordable online printers.

3. Think of a great reason why somebody would want to join your email list. If you want to 'gift' your patrons by offering them a free drink or a free dessert or a $5 Gift Certificate to join your email list…go for it. But you can also tell your patrons this, *"I have recently started an email newsletter for all of our guests. Free to join. I will send you information about all our events and promotions; plus when we add new dishes, new drinks or wines to our menu, you will be the first one to know. I would love for you to join so you are never missing out on any events that we will be doing in the future."*

4. When they fill out the card and give you their first name and email address at the end of night, have somebody enter all the names and addresses in your Constant Contact account. There is a video at TheFullRestaurantBook/ActionPlan that explains how to easily do this.

5. Your guests that join your email list will get a confirmation email from Constant Contact asking them to opt-in to your newsletter/email list. That insures that you are never ever accused of SPAM. Once they click on the link, they are done and are now part of your email list.

Promote Your Email Signup Aggressively

It pains me greatly when I see sharp entrepreneurs treat their email signup shabbily. Make your email signups difficult or painful to do and rest assured that you and your best friends will be the only subscribers you will ever see in the next decade. Here are two tips to make your email list grow fast:

- If you have a website, put a huge button on your home page asking your website visitors to sign up. Read the chapter on Local Search Marketing by Jacqueline Shaffer so you can start getting local clicks coming to your website. Maximize these clicks by building an email list from them.

- If you already put up a Facebook Page and believe me, you will once you read that chapter on Facebook Marketing by Urvi Mehta, ask your Facebook Fans to join your email list.

POWER TIP: USE AN EMAIL MARKETING SERVICE

What you don't want is an Excel spreadsheet with hundreds of email addresses. Use an email marketing service like Constant Contact to collect all the email addresses from day one. Not from day ten. Not from day one hundred. You never want to be accused of SPAM, nor should you waste time trying to cut and paste these email addresses every time you want to send an email out.

Instead go to TheFullRestaurantBook/ConstantContact and watch a short video and signup for the free trial. That will ensure that all email addresses are stored correctly from day one and that you are only one click away from sending your list a quick update.

Pictures, Pictures, Pictures

You are in the kitchen. Service is slowing down as the dinner rush eases into dessert and coffee. You see a gorgeous NY Strip land on the pass waiting for the server to pick up and be taken to its table. You grab your digital camera (which is always in your pocket) or your cell phone (which you know has a good camera) and snap a picture of that steak.

Next morning, before you start the day at your restaurant, you write a quick email which says, "A gorgeous NY Strip is a good thing to see and eat. Got this picture last night just before this steak went to its table. Hope you have as much fun looking at it as I did."

Attach the picture and hit SEND.

Restaurant owners are lucky as they have access to some beautiful images every day their restaurant is open. Instead of killing yourself trying to come up with paragraphs to fill your emails and newsletters – use pictures. Lots of them.

Best part about pictures: you take them once and then you use them over and over again. One good picture could be emailed, put on Twitpic, and uploaded to your Facebook Page. You want foodies to like you and talk about your restaurant? Foodies like food pictures. You want people to share your restaurant information between their Facebook friends – well, what do you think gets shared, clicked on, and commented on the most on Facebook? Nothing beats pictures.

How To Take Good Pictures In 60 Seconds

First, get yourself a decent slim camera. I stress slim because then you will carry it on you all the time. Don't obsess over megapixels; you won't be able to email really high resolution pictures in email anyway. A 4-5 Megapixel under $100 works just as good for your purposes as an $800 camera. If you have bought a cell phone in the last 12 months or you have a Blackberry or an iPhone, you already have a good camera. Take a couple of test pictures from your cell phone, transfer them to your computer or email them to yourself and see how they look on the computer screen. If they look appetizing, keep using your cell phone.

The best place to shoot your food is in your kitchen, as it is well lit. Put the plate on the counter and take a close up of the food. I put up some examples of food pictures that I have taken just for fun at my friends' restaurants and they actually end up using all of them in their Facebook and email marketing. Go to TheFullRestaurntBook.com/ActionPlan and check them out.

Sending Emails That People Share

We are living a revolution in word of mouth marketing. Tools like Facebook, Twitter, and Yelp have given tremendous power to a restaurant to put their food and their brand in front of thousands of potential diners with no advertising cost, just an investment of your time.

Every part of my online action plan for your restaurant is to teach you to stop thinking ONE TO ONE and start thinking SHARING.

Think about it this way – you can send an email out to the 200 people who are on your email list right now OR you can send an email out that these 200 people will be compelled to share with their friends. Let's say only 100 of these people open your email and read it, but then they immediately turn around and forward the email to 100 of their friends. Your restaurant just got a positive mention to 1000 people; 900 of them probably have never heard of your restaurant.

But sharing does not happen by itself. It happens when you encourage it. Two strategies to add share ability to your emails:

1. If you are sending a coupon out for an upcoming promo to your email list – let's say a special event you are doing for St. Patrick's Day – special hours, green beer and stuffed cabbage, and you want a house full restaurant throughout the day, don't write a text email because text is hard to share. Don't send a PDF version of your event flyer because PDFs are hard to share on Facebook and not easy to read on your cell phone. Instead, turn your flyer into an image because people love sharing images on Facebook and Twitter. The entire thing takes an extra three minutes to do:

   a. Create your flyer in MS-Word or Publisher like you would usually do.

   b. Go to http://JingProject.com and download Jing, free software that lets you capture any part of your screen and turn into an image with one click.

   c. Preview your flyer. Fire up Jing and take a snapshot of your screen and SAVE it. There, you just converted your flyer into an image.

   d. Email the flyer with a short, two line email.

2. Ask for people to share your promotions to your friends. Everybody loves sharing a great deal or an upcoming event. But most people never ask, so people might assume that you don't want everybody to know. After all, who would mind going to a restaurant and seeing some of their friends also hanging out there and having a good time?

More Viral

Sign off every email with a Call to Action. Here are three. Don't dump all three at the same time in one email. Use one at a time:

1. Link to your YELP review page (read the chapter on Yelp and you will be rushing to use this powerful, sometime scary website for marketing your restaurant). Ask nicely to have your restaurant rated on YELP.

2. Link to your Facebook Page (read the chapter on Facebook Page and set it up; you will be amazed at the results you will get out of it) and ask your email list to "LIKE YOU UP" on Facebook.

3. Link to your Twitter account (read the chapter on Twitter and set it up; this powerful, short messaging service will make word of mouth marketing work for you) and ask them to follow you on Twitter to get short and timely updates about your daily specials and upcoming events.

How To Write A Delicious Email Newsletter Every Month Without Stress

Don't feel bad. Even chain restaurants with 15 employees working full time in their online marketing department complain all day long about the *pressures* of writing an email newsletter every month. Most restaurant owners will look at you incredibly if you mention sending a newsletter out once a month. "But I am not a writer and who has time to sit and write an email newsletter?"

First of all, I am not asking you to create a literary masterpiece that might one day win the James Beard Award for Restaurant Email Newsletters. We are doing it to remind our past guests that we are alive and well, that our place is a great place to eat, that we have new and fun things going on, and that they should put our restaurant back on their *eating out* calendar for the month.

A Plan For You To Get Into The <u>Habit</u> Of Sending Out A Great Email Newsletter Every Month On Schedule

1. Use a service like Constant Contact so you don't have to stress over the technical part of making a nice email newsletter. Let me repeat, a law firm can get away with sending an all text email newsletter about the upcoming legislation changes that might affect its clients, but a restaurant cannot. Your email newsletter needs to look gorgeous, a feat that would have been hard to do a couple of years ago without hiring a HTML professional, but thanks to a service like Constant Contact, now you can send out beautiful and professional email newsletters without knowing one line of HTML.

2. Don't waste time trying to create a new design for your newsletter. Constant Contact has tons of ready to use email templates for you to click and use, so you can get this newsletter out on time.

3. Have a date every month to get the newsletter done and emailed. Deadlines make the world go around. Planes take off because they have to leave at their departure time. This is all about getting finished and hustling it out the door.

4. Use pictures. Lots of them. Of everything you can get a hold of. Staff, you, guests, food, kitchen, parties, and then use these pictures. A hard drive is no place to store pictures. Use every picture you have.

5. Can you think of one month which has no HOLIDAY or EVENT going on in a restaurant life? Valentine's Day, St. Patrick's Day, Mother's Day, Father's Day...the list goes on. Dedicate a place on your email newsletter to the upcoming event or holiday in the coming month and whatever you are planning to do that day. Open early, special brunch, green beer...there is something you intend to do that day and this is the place to inform your email list about it. That is also why it is important you send these newsletters out every month on a schedule so your guests know what you are doing for the upcoming month.

6. Just like cooking, you only become better at it if you do it. Take great pride in sending out a beautiful email newsletter every month because this is your business.

When Stalling... Get Somebody To Push You

Do you run your restaurant with a partner or your significant other? Sit down with them and tell them that it is really important for you personally, and for your business to thrive that you take this online marketing + email newsletter thing seriously. Tell them it is their responsibility to keep you in check and make sure that you are sending the emails out. They don't have to write them; just make sure that you are doing it.

ACTION PLAN

1. Go to TheFullRestaurantBook.com/ConstantContact for a quick tutorial on how to use the service for your restaurant and sign up for the free trial Download and print the email capture cards at TheFullRestaurantBook.com/ActionPlan

2. Talk to you servers and wait staff and start to capture your guests' email addresses beginning tonight.

3. Decide today on a **DATE** that you will send your email list a monthly newsletter.

4. Take ten pictures. Staff. Kitchen. Food. Guests. Restaurant. That is ten emails right there. All of a sudden, it does not look that complicated, does it?

5. Send me your first email. Send it in the morning and you will hear from me before the day is over. Send it at night and I will give you a shout out in the evening. My personal email is mark@thefullrestaurantbook.com.

6. Same thing with the newsletter. Once you are done with it, ship your first copy to mark@thefullrestaurantbook.com. I want to see it.

7. My email address mark@thefullrestaurantbook.com is the first one you should add to your Constant Contact list so I will get all your future email updates. Nothing would make me happier than to see that you are implementing the lessons learned from this book.

CHAPTER 11
Lights. Camera. Action!
Using Online Video To Fill Up Your Restaurant
by Mark Ijlal

"Hey, we are coming to Detroit from Chicago for a wedding on Sunday and would love to come to your place for the rehearsal dinner. We have around 25 people in our party."

"Oh wow, no problem, how did you hear about us in Chicago, if you don't mind me asking?"

"We saw your video about your restaurant on YouTube and man, let me tell you, that chicken dish that your chef was making in that video made all of us hungry. Can't wait to come there and eat that."

This is a real conversation that happened at a little family owned, great Italian restaurant called Maisano's Italian Restaurant in Novi, Michigan. The last five years have been tough on Metro Detroit restaurants. Despite a recession that hit Michigan double hard as the State took a hit from the global meltdown, and also from the auto industry crashing and burning all around it, Maisano's has done well for itself. By piggybacking on a combination of unbelievable food, great service, owners Michael and Leena who love making sure that every guest is having the best possible time every night, and of course, savvy online marketing that includes Facebook Pages, excellent reviews on Yelp and Yahoo Local, nosebleed local search rankings on Google and yes, an online video that has literally compelled people to drive 60 miles to eat their famous chicken marsala.

Online video is one of the biggest forces in Internet Marketing right now and yet very few restaurants use it to market their restaurants. This chapter will teach you everything you need to know on how to use online video, even though right now you may not even own a digital video camera.

YouTube For Restaurants

Many online video websites exist that let you upload and share video with people from all over the world. YouTube is the biggest of all, serving over 1,000,000,000 videos every single day to a worldwide audience. Then there are many smaller video sharing websites: Viddler.com, Vimeo.com, Blip.TV and a good two dozen more.

They all work the same:

- You create a free account by picking up a username, which for a business, is typically their name and a password.

- You upload a video you have either shot yourself or hired a professional to do for you.

- Within minutes the video is online. You can make it private or let the whole world watch it. You also have a couple of lines of HTML code that you can cut and paste anywhere to display your video along with a direct link to the video that you can email or embed on your Facebook Page.

That is pretty much all you need to know to get started in the world of online videos.

Oh, also, all these online video services are free. You are not paying anything for hosting the video, the software that converts the video into an online compatible format, or for the computer

142

power that is required to play back one or thousands of instances of the time the video is played. It is all free. No cost to you.

Cook It Myself Or Hire A Pro Chef?

The #1 question that restaurant owners ask me all the time is: should I do these videos myself or should I hire a professional videographer?

The answer is: you need to do both and here is why.

The Rockstar Video

You need to hire a professional videographer to create a 2-3 minute short film about your restaurant. Go to TheFullRestaurantBook.com/ActionPlan and check out the two restaurant videos. I call these videos the RockStar videos for restaurants. They are professionally shot with expensive cameras, perfect light and sound, and crisply edited with music. They are your first impression on people who just found your website or landed on your Facebook Page from Yelp, or just stumbled into your YouTube video via Google. It is going to cost you a couple of hundred dollars, but don't let your investment scare you. Unless you are planning a complete remodeling of your restaurant exterior and going from selling Italian food to being a Chinese takeout place – these videos will last you forever. Think of them as your signage. Do them once and they will continue to bring you business for a long time.

Short and with *hooks*:

Your guests' attention online is short. Like really short. Two minutes. You bore them and they are gone to someplace else more interesting.

143

You need what the song writers in Nashville would call a *hook*. Something that grabs the attention of the audience and keeps it there. They are not easy to figure out in songs. A great songwriter and producer would go through a mountain of hooks before finding the one that is worthy of building a hit song.

You, as a restaurant owner, have a gift when it comes to your *hook* that you can use online to draw more quality guests to you – it is called your *"signature dish."*. That dish that you are famous for. The one your regular patrons order all the time. The dish you recommend to all your new guests. Make that dish *THE HOOK* of your online video promotion.

Look closely at the Maisano's video again. Chicken Marsala, the dish for which they are already famous, is the center of attraction for the 2-minute video along with the owner of the restaurant, Michael. One of the things Michael and Leena hear most often is, "I want to eat that dish you are making in the video."

The Reality Tv Videos

You are in the kitchen. It is a busy Friday night and the dinner service is slowly winding down. It is noisy outside which makes you happy inside. A server walks up to you grinning and says the party of eight who are just finishing up dinner want to thank the restaurant owner for having an absolute blast here. You walk out and on your way you grab your Flip video camera. As you approach the table and introduce yourself, and before anybody starts talking, you say, *"Do you mind if get your feedback about our restaurant on my little Flip here – I would love to put that up on our Facebook Page if that is okay with all of you?"* And when they shout sure, go ahead, you smile and turn the camera on, point it to the smiling faces sitting around the table and say, *"So I hear*

144

that you guys are having a good time tonight..."

There are so many times in your restaurant life that the best moments will happen unscripted and unannounced. Twenty years ago, no business owner in their right mind could have even thought about shooting an *unprofessional video*: unedited, unscripted, unprepared, shot with a $50 camera or with a cell phone, and then put it up for the whole world to see.

But that was before Survivor and The Real World changed the way America watches TV. And now a Flipcam video is the one that goes viral and gets 40 million views instead of some polished video with a $300,0000 production value. Later in this chapter I am going to give a list of videos that you can shoot yourself with a $50 camera that will become some of the biggest drivers to fill your restaurant every night.

I Got Some Videos...Now What

1. Put your videos on Facebook. Videos are made for sharing. You can shoot a video of your chef making a new salad that you just started serving, turn around, connect your Flip to your laptop and have that video on your Facebook Page up and running in less than ten minutes. People like watching videos on Facebook, but Facebook also makes sharing that video literally a one-click thing.

2. Put it on YouTube and send the link to the video (cut and paste the link from your Internet browser) to your email list.

3. Embed the video in your website, on the Home Page so nobody can ever miss it. When I see a gorgeous video hidden somewhere on a website under the boring title of

About Us or Tour Our Restaurant, I wonder if the restaurant owner understands how much business they are not getting because they are not leveraging this great asset to its fullest extent.

Why Do You Need A Pro Videgrapher?

There is Chinese restaurant in my hometown that runs local cable television ads during weekends. I am not sure if the production company has problems with their equipment or the problem is with the restaurant, because their food looks horrible in their TV ads. Bad to the point where I don't want to go there and eat.

But I don't think that their problem is with the food. It is the way it is being shot. I see the same thing on most restaurant websites. If they are using pictures of the food they serve – the pictures are really bad. But then you look at Gourmet or Food & Wine magazine and you literally want to eat the magazine by itself because the food looks so good.

There is a reason for this – shooting food, whether for still photography or video, is different than shooting a person or a building.

Food has many colors and needs an experienced professional who actually knows how to shoot food because believe it or not, a whole specialty of professionals do just that for a living. You can't just hand a $100 camera to a member of your wait staff and expect the resulting video to look like an episode of Food Network, but that is how it is supposed to look.

People watching anything to do with food online have certain expectations. They have not seen your food up close before but they have seen videos on TV before. That is the mental picture they have.

Before You Hire A Pro

Ask them if they have done a video for a local small business before. If they have, you want to see a sample of their work.

Watch the two videos on TheFullRestaurantBook.com/ActionPlan. You want a video that is comparable or even better. Don't compromise on this. This is your first impression video and you will not be changing it everyday.

Ask for references from their past clients. At least three names and phone numbers and then call all three, one by one and ask them about their experience with the videographer – were they happy, did they finish on time, did they show up on time, and would they consider using them for future projects?

Use Craigslist for finding videographers under Gigs/Creative section. Run a small advertisement (it is free) and you will get 10-15 videographers emailing you immediately who would be happy to deliver a video like this to you. Show them the videos on our website and ask for a quote.

Before You Hire Yourself:

1. You need a good camera. Most digital cameras nowadays come with a digital video feature. I shot over 200 videos with a $130 camera I bought from Costco and it worked great. If you bought a digital camera in the last twelve months, chances are pretty good that your camera can shoot excellent indoor video.

2. You can buy a dedicated video camera; something small like Flip or its HD cousins are pretty good, small, and under $150 in most configurations. And you can always use it to shoot your home and vacation videos.

3. The difference between amateur and professional video is all to do with light and sound. A professional videographer will know how to manipulate light and use professional microphones to create production quality sound. You, on the other hand, have to do with what you have. But you are in luck since these short videos are not that audio heavy, meaning you are not chatting away for 20 minutes. You want to keep them at two minutes at most. Getting great light for your videos is easy since every restaurant kitchen in America is brightly lit with fluorescent lights, which are more than enough to create passable videos for Facebook and YouTube.

4. The best advice I can give you for putting out great videos about your restaurant is: don't take it too seriously because when you do, you will freeze, think about it too much, and in the end either do nothing (because you are still thinking about it) or be unhappy about anything you do shoot. It is two minutes. Get it done and as long as it is good enough, get it out there. This is not about shooting, editing, and making it perfect. This is about shooting and uploading it.

Teach The World What You Know

Here are ten videos that any restaurant owner can make with a $50 Flip camera attached to a $20 tripod and upload them to YouTube. The videos could be two minutes in length. No fancy titles or special effects needed. Modify the list to suit your own menu and drop me an email with a link to the videos you end up doing out of this list at mark@thefullrestaurantbook.com.

1. What do you like better: fresh pasta or dry pasta?

2. Which cut of steak is your favorite and why?

3. When you go out to eat at other restaurants, what is the first thing you notice?

4. The rules of red wine (goes with meat, etc.) and why you should break them.

5. The rules of white wine (goes with seafood & chicken) and why you should break them.

6. What is the most loved and most ordered dish in your restaurant and where did the recipe come from?

7. What was your favorite dish growing up that mom, grandma or dad made that you have never forgotten?

8. The best meal you ever had.

9. The chef that completely blows your mind and why?

10. Why homemade burgers never taste as good as restaurant cooked, and how you can make your next burger much better.

The Secret Behind Great Online Videos

I have done around 300 online videos. Although none of them went viral and got 10 million views, they collectively brought my company a tremendous amount of new and good business. Here are some of the biggest lessons I have learned from doing online videos for my own business:

1. It is not about the camera. It is not the day of the week. It is not about whether it is a sunny day outside or a cloudy one. It is not even as much as about the content of the video. It helps that you are knowledgeable about the topic but it will not make the video achieve the results you want for your restaurant by itself. So if you understand a lot about wine, that is good and you should be doing videos about wine, but you don't have to be a professional sommelier to talk about which red wine should go well, in your opinion, with a NY Strip steak.

2. It is about passion. Passion comes from talking about things that you care about deeply. If you really don't care about wine and you are a beer drinker every day, then skip doing wine videos and do five videos about your favorite beer and why people should not just be ordering the same old beer every time they go out.

3. Add new faces sometimes. Get your wine rep to join forces with you and do some videos in which he or she teaches you about wine.

4. It is about personality. If you can laugh from the heart and it seems that you actually care about sharing what you know about food and wine and everything else that goes on in your restaurant, your audience is smart enough to realize that this is fun stuff to watch and share. *"Wanting to be someone else is a waste of the person you are."* Kurt Cobain said that and it is worth remembering when you sit in front of the camera and the red light comes on.

ACTION PLAN

1. Go to TheFullRestaurantBook.com/ActionPlan and check out some of the restaurant videos that we have put together for you as samples.

2. Run an ad on Craigslist to hire a local pro.

3. Get your RockStar video done.

4. Upload the video to YouTube.

5. Embed the video in your website.

6. Put the video on your Facebook Page.

7. Email everybody in your list with the link to the video.

8. Get a Flipcam or check if your digital camera can shoot decent video.

9. Buy a tripod and an external microphone if your digital camera supports it.

10. Shoot one video every week at your restaurant and distribute it everywhere you are putting your restaurant online. Facebook and your website should be on top of your list.

CHAPTER 12
You Got A NEW TEXT MESSAGE!
by Mark Ijlal

I speak on a regular basis at conferences and seminars about online marketing. Sometimes I will get approached during a break or after my presentation is over by a restaurant owner who will say something like, "Okay, I get what you are talking about Facebook and Twitter and Local Search but, but, but, I just cannot do any of the above for various reasons so WHAT CAN I DO NOW till I get my act straightened out and get serious about online marketing?"

This chapter is about WHAT YOU CAN DO NOW...

This is my answer to these folks: "Start collecting cell phone numbers and learn how to text your promotions in 160 characters or less in a way that will compel your previous guests to revisit your restaurant again in the next 48 hours."

Do You Run A Sport Bar Or Gastro Pub?

You can literally change your restaurant revenue numbers in 60 days just by implementing this step in my online action plan. Almost all sports bars & gastro pubs run some sort of promotion on slow days: cheap beer and chicken wings are two that come to mind above everything.

Yes, you can send emails about these nights and promotions, but a lot of these *'Let's go to the sport bar'* type decisions are made on the spur of the moment, while people are leaving the office. You can send them an email, and you should if you have built an email list, but you can't beat the urgency of a text message.

You text them. They receive it in the next 30 seconds and it will be read in the next 15 seconds and a decision will be made to come to your place tonight or keep on driving. But it is instant and it is perfect for filling up a slow night.

Text Messaging Is Different

Do you remember the days when cell phones came out and how excited you were when your phone rang? How about voice mail? Ever stopped doing what you were doing so you could listen to your cell phone voice mail messages around five years ago? You are not alone. We all did. But everything gets old and now when we see six voice mail messages on our cell phone, we are not in a rush to listen to them immediately. Same thing with email. If you open your Inbox and there are thirteen new emails, you will skim most and read the ones NOW that are from family, your business partner, or your best friend and the rest will be looked at sometime later.

But when somebody texts you, even now, what do you do? The cell phone says NEW TEXT MESSAGE and you immediately hit OK to read the text message, no matter what you are doing. There is a reason why most States are banning driving and texting because people just cannot wait, not even for a red light, to read or respond to their text messages even at the cost of risking their lives.

Everybody has a cell phone. Everybody has a text message plan. Some have unlimited text plans. Some have 250-1000 text messages per month text plans, but I rarely find somebody nowadays who cannot receive text messages on their cell phones.

"But I Never Text Anybody"

I have been building a permission list of my clients to text them occasionally for four years now and they are all very happy that my company reminds them of important events so they don't miss out on anything. I actually just got an email from a client 20 minutes ago, just before I started writing this chapter. He has been with me for five years now and wanted to know if he has given me his new cell phone number because he just noticed that he has not been getting any text messages from my company in the last 60 days.

Look, the worst mistake any business owner can make is to impose our way of doing things on our customers. This is self sabotage of good online marketing of the worst kind. "I don't want to do this because I don't use this personally." That is like saying that unless you personally love every dish in your restaurant, you would not serve it. And you and I both know that is not true. Most chefs think that Filet Mignon is a lame cut of meat and prefer eating a bone-in NY Strip or Rib Eye steak. Bone and fat make the steak go around to experienced palates. But the public loves Filet Mignon so every steak house in the land – chain or independent – serves Filet Mignon.

Text messaging is not going anywhere soon. Your customers will love you for reminding them of great promotions in a timely manner and you will get the proof of that when they show up at your restaurant tonight after you have sent them a text message.

How You Can Use Text Messaging To Fill Up Your Restaurant Tonight

1. Start building a list of cell phone numbers from guests coming to your restaurant, sports bar, and gastro pub tonight.

2. The list is *permission-based*: you are going to disclose upfront why you are asking for their phone numbers and what they can expect. Meaning, your wait staff will be saying something like: "We text our guests once a week when we have a special promotion going on: cheap drinks, $2 beer, game night promotions. If you want to join our cell phone texting list – just fill out this little card and leave it on the table. If at any time you want us to stop texting you – you can unsubscribe right from your cell phone."

3. There is a sample card that you can use to do step #2 on TheFullRestaurantBook.com/ActionPlan . Download it and print it.

4. Sign up with a text messaging service. We have a list on our website.

5. Compose your first text message about a *special* you want to do tonight.

6. Hit SEND.

160 Characters Or Less

Text messaging is about getting to the point immediately because you are limited to 160 characters. You cannot send one message broken over three separate text messages. That will annoy everybody. If you have something long to say – say it via email or on your Facebook Page.

Texting is for letting your customers know about a specific promotion that is going on tonight or tomorrow night. That is it. Think of it as a short coupon ad. Once you write it, read it aloud to your wait staff or whoever is around and ask them what they understood from the short message. If their understanding matches your intent...you are good to go.

So, here is the recipe for a good text message:

1. It is an announcement. You just opened up a new location, remodeled, redid the menu, new beer came in the market; all good reasons to shout out a text tonight.

2. It is a coupon. $2 Beers and all you can eat wings on game night or $2 martinis during happy hours also make good text messages.

3. Track what you are sending out. If you start doing lots of text campaigns and want to see what is working the best, instead of just blasting a text message and telling everybody to come on in, insert a code in the text message – HAPPY could be the code to get $2 martinis and tell your guests to tell your server the code. Change your POS so the only way your server can ring up a $2 martini that day is to type in that code. At the end of the day you can see how many customers your text message campaign brought in. Do it often and you will start seeing patterns on what really works.

4. It should have an expiry date. Text messages are about NOW. Ideally, the text message you are shipping out at 3pm is about something you are doing tonight. Keep it about something you are doing tonight and tomorrow night but stop at that. It cannot be about a promo that will last for a month. You want to use text messages to create a rush to your front door tonight. Every other event or promotion needs to go via Facebook or email.

Sign Up With A Text Messaging Service

1. There are many text messaging services that let you upload a list of cell phone numbers in a Microsoft Excel or text file, type a short message and hit SEND, and everybody on the list gets your text within 60 seconds or so. You don't need to know what cell phone carriers these phone numbers belong to. The online service texts everybody regardless of what carriers these phone numbers belong to.

2. I have provided a list of text messaging service providers at TheFullRestaurantBook.com/ActionPlan. They differ a little bit on pricing but almost all of them charge a small monthly fee: $10 to $15, and then you pay for each text message you send out. The rates differ, but they are, in all cases, a couple of cents per text message.

Very Important: Unsubscribe Requests

This is a permission-based list; your guests have graciously given you permission to inform them about your restaurant promotions and events. Just like an email marketing campaign which always has an option to opt-out or stop receiving future emails from a business, all text messaging companies give an option of hitting a key or two that will send you a message informing you that your customer does not wish to receive any more text messages from you.

Please pay attention to these requests and delete these numbers from your cell phone list immediately. You never ever want to be accused of SPAM. That is terrible word of mouth marketing. Most text messaging services automatically unsubscribe these requests from your list. Ask them to make sure that you don't have to do anything from your end to make this happen.

How Often Should You Text?

Avoid the temptation of texting every night to inform that your restaurant is OPEN and what is on your daily special menu. For that, you have your Facebook Page and your Twitter account.

I recommend slow nights. Let's say your Tuesdays are a slow night every week like clockwork. Make Tuesday noon your text-time for running a promo to bring some feet through the door.

Encourage Forwarding

I doubt that there is a cell phone in the world right now with an empty Contact book. Everybody has stored phone numbers in their cell phone. How many times recently have you gotten a family picture or some news forwarded to you by somebody close to you?

New customers equal new revenue for your restaurant. So

when you are texting your guest list, encourage forwarding in the message.

Instead of saying "$2 Martinis Happy Hour at Angelo's, 37468 Garden Way in Downtown Cleveland," text "Come with good friends tonight to Angelo's for $2 Martinis and happy times – 37468 Garden Way, 44115."

If you are texting an EVENT like NBA, NFL, or NHL game night promotions, writing the text to encourage your guests to forward is even more important. Obviously, 160 characters doesn't give you too much room to say that in detail, but cut on the hype. 'Best chicken wings in Cleveland' can be deleted in favor of "Fwd this text to your friends."

ACTION PLAN

1. Download and print the card template from TheFullRestaurantBook.com/ActionPlan.

2. Start handing it out to guests every night and start building your cell phone list.

3. Sign up with a text messaging service. I have a list at TheFullRestaurantBook.com/ActionPlan.

4. Send your first text message.

CHAPTER 13
You will be YELPED!
by Mark Ijlal

"We found your restaurant on Yelp."

"Oh My God. Somebody just trashed my restaurant on Yelp."

What Ever Happened To That Website?

Once upon a time, there was a thing called The Internet. Small and big businesses made things called websites where they would tell the world what their business was all about and once the website was up, most of them decided that they could go back to doing what they were doing before this pesky Internet thing came along and they would never have to worry about online marketing.

That plan worked for about ten years and then something crazy started happening. Millions and then hundreds of millions of people decided that just watching a video or reading a news report on the Internet was not enough. They actually wanted to *share* what they thought of that video or that TV show or a local restaurant at which they ate last night with the rest of the world. Not just with friends or mom but with the rest of the world.

If Web 1.0 for a business was about building a website and then doing nothing, Web 2.0 is about people like the four-topper that you just served 30 minutes ago letting you know what they thought about your food, your service, and your restaurant.

Over the last five years, YouTube, Facebook, Flickr, and MySpace have become THE INTERNET for millions of people in the same way that email and surfing defined the Internet for millions for a good ten years. The genie was out of the bottle and it was not going back. Ever.

True review websites have existed for decades in newspapers (NY Times restaurant review) and in book form (Zagat), but now anybody could walk into your restaurant, take pictures of the food as it is being served, write a four line review about the food on her iPhone, and post it to Yelp by the time the coffee came around.

And there is absolutely nothing you can do to stop her.

This is probably one of the most important chapters in my online action plan for restaurant owners. It is not just about another marketing tool to employ, but rather the biggest shift in online marketing which is fast moving from traditional advertising to 'word of mouth marketing.' It is also important because it will force you to deal with some unpleasant things like reading a negative review, and I am going to be blunt about what you can do if it ever happens to your restaurant.

What Is Yelp?

Yelp is a website where customers can talk about and rate local small businesses. And when I say 'talk,' I mean it. Here is how Yelp describes itself on their website: 'Yelp is the fun and easy way to find, review, and talk about what's great – and and not so great – in your area.'

Who Are Yelpers?

Your customers, your competitor's customers, and your family members are on Yelp. They are writing about the great meal they had last night when they went out to celebrate dad's birthday and they are also writing about the plumber who showed up two hours late, never offered an explanation or apology, and then left dirty footprints all over the new carpet despite being asked to be careful. They live in California and in Kansas. They are men and women, young and old, kind and skeptic, generous and sometimes harsh.

In fact, Yelp is a lot like you and me. It is made up of real people sharing their real experiences.

But, But, Do I Have To Be On Yelp?

Why can't we just turn off Yelp? Can't you write an email to Yelp informing them of your decision that you choose not to participate in their review website and that you'd rather be left alone?

Well, the answer is NO. Customers have the right to talk about what they like and don't like about a business. As Yelp says on its website:

"The law is clear on this point — even if you've registered your business name as a trademark — so your best bet is to engage with your fans and critics alike, and hear what they have to say."

Is Yelp Against Restaurant Owners?

Actually, no. Yelp gives business owners some great tools, for free, to manage their restaurant name and reputation; and at the same time, Yelp can drive new customers to you in your city, people who have never heard of your restaurant before. All for free.

Once you have set up your business owner account and verified that you are who you are by getting a code via phone call to your business phone, you can do a whole lot of things quickly to make your restaurant stand out in the sea of other restaurants in your city

162

whose owners are not using Yelp in their online marketing.

You can:

- Describe your restaurant cuisine and specialties, etc.

- Add location hours, payment methods, accessibility options.

- Add photos to make your listing attractive.

- Announce promotions.

- Point to upcoming events.

- Track how many people view your business page.

- Email your customers who are using Yelp, both publicly and privately.

Why Can't I Just Call 10 Of My Family Members To Write Fake Reviews On Yelp For My Restaurant?

No kidding, I have been asked this question more than once. Well, you can't. I will give you three good reasons why this is a bad idea, and as somebody who uses Yelp a lot to visit new restaurants, I am your customer so you should listen carefully to what I am about to tell you about fake reviews.

1. It is unethical.

2. Yelp has some extremely smart people working for them who have created sophisticated software to review and remove fake reviews. Think how Google is able to spot SPAM websites pretty easily. Yelp knows that a very small percentage of restaurant owners might, in their

shortsightedness, try to pull this off and they routinely review and remove fake reviews. You are better off spending this energy in making your Yelp listing look awesome.

3. When I am reading a review about a restaurant that has been given great ratings by a Yelper and the review is talking about the 'great food' or 'incredible service' – my eyes always wander first to the number of reviews that this Yelper has written, which is displayed right underneath the Yelper's name. Think about this for a minute: if you ask ten of your friends to write fake reviews for you, then how many reviews do you think will show up underneath their name? One to be exact. You can have ten reviewers with one review under their belt giving you five stars, and one of your competitors has two reviews only but both reviewers have 300 Yelp reviews underneath their name. Who do you think I will believe more?

Add Pictures

Yelp lets business owners and your customers upload pictures of the business they review or own. Millions of customers have uploaded pictures of restaurants, the food they were served (sometimes as it is being served to them, by taking a picture from their cell phone and uploading it instantly) and even taking a picture of the menu and putting it up on Yelp.

Restaurants are a picture friendly business. Do you know how hard it is to take pictures of a law office? Cubicles and phone systems really don't make that attractive a background.

Some tips:

1. For better or worse, your restaurant pictures form as strong an impression on a new customer as your reviews. Take this seriously.

2. If you are not good at taking pictures or don't own a decent camera – ask somebody else to help you. Family members, friends, wait staff – there has to be somebody there who can help you who owns a decent digital camera.

3. Hire a professional if you just simply cannot find anybody to help you out. Run an ad on your city's Craigslist by going to www.CraigsList.org in the Gigs/Creative section and ask for a photographer who has taken pictures of restaurants and food before.

4. Light. You need light. Take the pictures during daytime, pull the blinds back or turn all lights up when you are taking pictures of your restaurant interior. On Facebook, I just saw a restaurant video of a party. The entire thing was shot in complete darkness.

5. One or two pictures of an empty restaurant or bar are fine but what you really want are pictures of your guests having a good time. Ask for permission and tell them you will use these pictures for your website, Facebook, and Yelp. Some people may not want to be photographed and you have to respect their privacy wishes. Take pictures close to the table so the flash on your camera is more effective.

6. Not every dish looks great on the plate. Well, some look better than others. Take pictures in the well lighted kitchen. Go to TheFullRestaurantBook.com/ActionPlan and check

out some of the sample pictures I took just for fun with my camera.

7. Good mix: restaurant inside (empty), dinner time, lunch or breakfast (if you do them all), food, bar, wait staff group picture.

8. Take a big gulp and try to be, even though you may hate getting your picture taken, in as many pictures as possible. If you are shaking your head in vigorous denial, read the chapter on Lessons You Can Learn from Food Network before saying no.

Encourage Your Customers To Write Reviews About Your Restaurant

It is quite depressing to see a great restaurant at the bottom of a Yelp page because they have one review which was written three years ago. Yes, there are millions of passionate Yelp users but there are also millions of small businesses, including restaurant owners, and it may be a while before you accumulate 10-12 reviews.

I don't like waiting and neither should you.

Encourage your guests to write reviews about you if they already use Yelp. Don't ask them to write positive reviews. Just ask them nicely to share on Yelp what they have experienced with your restaurant.

I know what you are thinking. This is crazy, what if they say something nasty about your restaurant?

Well, if they are going to say something bad about your

restaurant, it is not like you can stop them from saying it, so why is this thought keeping you from getting 24 great reviews?

Come on. Have a little faith in your restaurant and in people. Nobody is getting up every morning with a mission of destroying you. People have enough going on in their lives as it is, to sit and plot the destruction of your restaurant.

What If Somebody Says Something Bad About Your Restaurant?

Although this chapter is about Yelp, the following tips apply to every aspect of your online marketing. Bad reviews do happen. They are not new, but previously, people who were unhappy with your restaurant could only tell their friends about the crummy service they got. Now, they get to tell the whole world on Facebook, Twitter, and Yelp.

Is it fair?

I mean, bad nights happen in the restaurant industry. Sometimes the food does not come out well despite your best intentions, you are short on wait staff, and it takes too long to get the food out; in short, like with any other business, sometimes you fail to meet your customer's expectations.

Do people sometimes unnecessarily write harsh reviews? Is it possible that they were having a bad night before they came to your restaurant and even a little mistake seems like a complete bomb to them?

Well, yes, and it has happened to you, me, and everybody else in this world. The social Internet is about people, and people are loving, caring, messy, angry, sad, and happy at times. So are you.

167

So, what can you do to make the most of your bad reviews?

1. Saying, "I am sorry that happened," and really meaning it goes a long way.

2. Don't pick a fight. Whether you are right or wrong – you will lose in the core of public opinion. The forums at Yelp are littered with business owners blowing their cool at negative reviews and saying nasty things about the reviewers only to see another 200 people comment on their craziness.

3. There is a link at TheFullRestaurantBook.com/ActionPlan that points to a recent Inc. magazine article on Yelp. Just read the first four paragraphs and you won't know whether to laugh or cry, but you will know why picking a public fight with a customer is not exactly a smart marketing move. I am not talking about legal issues here. I am not a lawyer. But I know beyond the shadow of a doubt that in the world we live in – fighting in a public forum is a bad idea no matter how justified you feel in your war.

4. It is unrealistic that all of your reviews will be 5 Stars. Everybody has a different personal palate about food. What you might think is an absolutely great dry rub for a steak might only taste okay to somebody else. I will even make an argument that a mix of reviews – some 5 stars, some 4 stars, some 3 stars and even a 2 star review – make your restaurant's overall ratings seem more genuine to a new customer. We are not fools. We are also not that harsh. I have gone dozens of times to a restaurant with a mix of ratings just because I read both the top and middle reviews and really didn't care about the reasons that prompted the

reviewers to give the restaurant 3 stars. The same way that I have bought dozens of books from Amazon.com with a middle of the line review.

5. Ask your restaurant's staff about that complaining customer or that particular night before you jump on Yelp to answer them. Is it possible that night was a busy night and their food was delayed for 40 minutes but you were busy in the front and nobody told you? Is it possible that they did send the steak back three times because it was undercooked the first time and cold the second time?

6. If all of your complaints are about ONE thing – maybe your customers are trying to tell you something. Maybe your reservation system is broken if all of your complaints are about having to wait for 30-45 minutes before being seated for dinner, and it is about time you do something about it. Maybe a large number of your wait staff during lunch are new at their jobs and keep screwing up orders and you need to take some time off to train them better.

7. Above all, keep your cool at all times.

8. Never write an email to anybody, ever, if you are having a bad day. Believe me, and I am telling you this from personal experience, you will regret it the next morning.

ACTION PLAN

1. Unlock your business listing by going to www.Yelp.com.

2. Scroll all the way down to the bottom of the page and click on *BUSINESS OWNERS.*

3. On the next page, click on Access Your Business Account.

4. Watch the short video Yelp has for business owners and click on Get Your Business Account.

5. Find your business. Fill out a simple form. Get a phone call to verify you are not trying to poach off somebody else's business and you are all set to go.

6. Upload pictures of your restaurant.

7. Take pictures of your menu and upload them.

8. Add as much information about your restaurant as you can.

CHAPTER 14
The Revolution Will Be iPhoned
by Mark Ijlal

I don't have to call anybody anymore to find a good restaurant. I can turn my iPhone on; it knows immediately where I am because of the GPS built right into it. I fire up an app like Urban Spoon, select the type of food I feel like eating and I shake my iPhone, and like a Las Vegas slot machine, Urban Spoon rolls its wheels and presents me with its choices, all with pictures and reviews from my fellow web surfers. If your restaurant is not found, chances are that I am not coming to your restaurant anytime soon.

In the first three months of 2010, Apple sold 8,750,000 iPhones. Since it launched two years ago, Apple has sold 51,500,000 iPhones and the tide continues to rise.

Once upon a time, people found new restaurants by asking their friends or by finding them in their local Yellow Pages or in little ads in the newspapers.

Now, people find new restaurants on Yelp, Urban Spoon, Yahoo Local, and more and more on their cell phones.

First things first...these are not phones, but rather small computers that also happen to dial out when you need them. In the next five years, the cell phone of the last decade, a small flip phone with a keypad and a little screen, will go the way of digital pagers. There was a time in America where 60,000,000 people carried pagers everyday. Now, the only people carrying pagers are doctors and information technology professionals on call who provide tech support to big companies.

Pagers are dead and gone and the non-smart cell phone, a little thing made to make phone calls, is about to go away too. All phones soon will be smart phones with high speed Internet access from anywhere, 24/7.

Think about this for a second: there are more mobile phones in the world than personal computers.

People don't sit in front of their computers 24/7, but everybody carries their cell phone with them 24/7. Most people can't even go for a walk without carrying their cell phone. Heck, most of my friends go to the bathroom and take their cell phone with them so they can check their emails, text somebody, or just play a quick game while they are answering nature's call.

How Can You Make Your Restaurant Show Up On Smart Phones?

The thing about being found on smart phones is that you don't have to do anything extra. If you implement everything I have written in the online action plan of this book – your restaurant will do well in showing up in mobile searches in your city.

1. Encourage your guests / Facebook fans to take pictures of your restaurant, the food they are eating and the good time they are having. People share the pictures that they take with their cell phones. Either they are going on their Facebook profile or if you ask them nicely they might even post them on your restaurant Facebook Page. The camera on a new iPhone is better than the $400 camera I bought last year. Most people don't carry digital cameras around. They don't have to. The cell phone is enough. One of the ways to encourage people is to notice the pictures that people upload to your Facebook Page, or comment on

Twitter about them. If you never say anything when people take time out of their extremely busy lives to brighten your Page – it says that you simply don't care and that is not a good message to send out. Comment, and you will get more.

2. Be alive and well on Yelp. Claim your listing. Write a good description of your restaurant. Upload pictures. Point your guests and everybody else you are connecting with online to write a review about you on Yelp. If your food and service are good then why aren't your customers talking about you? Yelp and Urban Spoon are two of the most popular, most downloaded apps at the iPhone store. Be wary of not showing up there.

3. Google Places: Read the chapter on Local Search Marketing and do step by step what Jacqueline Shaffer is suggesting to make sure that your Google Places listing is correct; have pictures and a pointer to your YouTube video. iPhone and Android phones both use Google Maps as a default application for directions. You want to be found at the top here. If your listing is claimed, updated, has pictures, coupons and updates – these are all signs to Google that your restaurant is alive and well.

4. Short Emails: A whole lot of your guests are checking their Inbox on their cell phones. Keep your emails short and to the point. Long winded emails and newsletters will get dumped to "I will read it later when I get home" – that day will never come as your email will be buried in an avalanche of more incoming emails by the time they get home. I have deleted thousands of emails in the last 12

months from my Inbox; so have you. Nobody has time to read every email that is coming to them.

5. Text Messages: If you are not doing anything else in your online marketing due to time constraints – you should be at least collecting cell phone numbers from your guests and texting those promotions, etc. on a regular basis. Read the chapter on Text Messaging.

6. YouTube Video: Google owns YouTube. iPhone ships with a YouTube app right on the first screen. Even if you are using a different service to play back your videos (Facebook, Vimeo, Viddler, Blip, private hosting account) you should be putting all your videos on a free YouTube account so your mobile phone users can easily watch any restaurant video you are putting out.

7. Facebook Page: The Facebook app on the iPhone is one of the most popular apps ever. That is not changing anytime soon. Facebook is becoming more serious about giving its business users better and smarter tools to manage Pages. Your future guests can check out your restaurant Facebook Page easily from the smart phones which become even more essential if you want your existing fans to recommend your Page to their Facebook Friends.

CHAPTER 15
Tracking Your Online Marketing
by Mark Ijlal

Peter Drucker, considered by many as one of the great business minds of all time, once said, *"What gets measured, gets improved."*

But what do you measure when you already have 10,000 fires to put out everyday as a restaurant owner? Count 15,000 fires if you are also the chef in your restaurant kitchen. If you are going to spend all your free time analyzing your online marketing activity, then what time exactly are you going to spend running your restaurant?

The easy thing for me is to play Monday morning quarterback and tell you that you need to focus on online marketing and running your business should be secondary. That is a piece of advice that marketing consultants love giving out. Obviously, in their worlds there are no employee or vendor problems, every customer is completely in love with your product, and you don't have a family or life outside of work. So at 2am, you should not be sleeping after a 14-hour workday, but rather answering your emails.

It is a good piece of advice that never gets implemented in the real world. So I don't want you to track everything in online marketing right now, only enough that will help you get more guests to your restaurant and know that you are on the right track.

1. The most important thing to know right now: Tracking something is not about doing it for the first 48 hours, but doing it continuously until you have a clear picture on what

is working best for your restaurant. If you send a promotional email out and you get 40 guests to come in the next two nights…that is pretty good, right? Well, it is but we don't know enough yet. What if we send another email two weeks from today and that offer gets 130 guests to come in the next three days…now which one is better?

Facebook Page: The number of fans, obviously, is important. If every week you have more fans due to either word of mouth advertising from your existing fans who like sharing your pictures, videos, and short updates with their friends, you are doing great. More importantly you need to go into Facebook Insights – a tracking tool that Facebook provides to its Page Administrators to see what is going on behind the scenes.

Look at your Pages and see how many fans have unsubscribed – meaning how many people who at one time liked your Page enough to keep in touch with your updates have now told Facebook to 'hide' your future updates from them. If that number is rising every day – you are boring your fans. Simple as that. People don't want to be bored on Facebook. There is enough of that already from TV ads and annoying junk mail coming to them. They will give you their attention and they will share your promotions back to their worlds, but in return they ask that you don't bore them. Let me give you an example – if all you ever do, every day is announce your daily special with a price, you are boring me. If you post a great picture of a steak instead you might even get me to write a comment on it. "This is making me hungry." I made a short video available at TheFullRestaurantBook.com/ActionPlan to show you how to get that report in Facebook in less than two minutes. You don't need to obsess over it everyday but you do need to watch it once a week.

2. Facebook will also send you a weekly report that will tell you three things: how many new people came to your Facebook and gave you permission to send them updates about your restaurant, how many people LIKED the different things you put out during the week, and how much people actually visited your Facebook Page. It would look something like this:

3. Your Guests Tonight: Train your wait staff to ask everybody casually, "Is this your first time here?" and if they answer yes, then ask them, "How did you find us?" Make a sheet with two columns – waiter initials and the answers. Do it for one week and you will start seeing what is working well for you and what is not. If 80% of online answers consist of Facebook and nothing else, or they are all coming there because they saw the video of the cowboy steak being made in your kitchen...you need to do more videos of your dishes and start dropping them on YouTube and Facebook.

4. Get your wait staff excited about online marketing. Tell them that the reason you are doing it is to bring more and better guests every night to the restaurant. They make their living off tips and nobody in their right mind would want to work in an empty restaurant. If you are going to complain loudly every day about spending five minutes to update your Facebook Page, your staff will only mirror your attitude about everything. There is an old political saying; people get the leaders that they deserve. Well, a business

culture or the way things are done when managers are not around, is about mirroring the attitude of the boss. Be excited about your online marketing; take great pride in the people who are finding you from your online marketing and your wait staff will reflect your attitude.

If you are emailing special offers or putting them out on Twitter – add little four digit codes to them so you can track what is coming back. Make a simple spreadsheet, I have a sample one at
TheFullRestaurantBook.com/ActionPlan
and track what is coming back so you always know what is working. The direct response marketing folks are always testing one piece of marketing against another to find what works really well. They call it your *control* piece and then everything else is tested against that.

CHAPTER 16
Building Online Buzz
by Mark Ijlal

"No news is good news." True or False?

It's an old saying that does not work anymore, for the restaurant business, at least. Why would you want a complete online silence about your restaurant? Do you want people to recommend you to their online Facebook friends and Twitter followers and blog readers?

Right now how many *'conversations'* are taking place about your restaurant online? Is somebody saying something nice about your fresh, handmade pasta right now? What about the new cowboy coffee-rubbed steak that has been getting rave reviews for the last three nights? What would your restaurant reservations look like tomorrow night if a couple thousand people who have never heard of your restaurant all of a sudden started hearing about it again and again?

Will that help you fill up your restaurant night after night without spending thousands every month in wasteful PR campaigns or sitting in a corner hoping that somebody from a local TV station will 'discover' you soon?

Come on…waiting is so highly overrated. If Brad Pitt can go to auditions before he became Brad Pitt, so can you. Don't wait for the world to come to you. Go to the world and show them that coffee-rubbed steak in all its bloody charbroiled glory.

You need more people in your restaurant. Let's go and talk to some folks who will help you to do just that.

Regulars Vs. The Influentials

Restaurants always had *'regulars'* – folks who showed up night after night or weekend after weekend and brought their friends and families. They were the local word of mouth marketing for a restaurant, and as its and the chef's reputation grew, they were all you needed.

It is a different world now. The *'regulars'* are still here and you should do whatever it takes to keep them happy because they are your champions and they love your restaurant and your food above all the choices they had tonight.

But there are other people in your town and in towns nearby who don't just talk to friends and families about how great George's new cowboy steaks are; they actually talk to hundreds and sometimes thousands of people who live locally. Let's call them *the influentials.*

The three most important of these *local influentials* for your restaurant are: active Twitter users, mommy bloggers, and the biggest, most important group of people who are spearing a movement in food journalism – local food bloggers.

Host Tweetups

When Twitter started gaining popularity, so did Tweetups, informal gatherings of people who found each other on Twitter and now want to meet face to face. Tweetups are not owned or managed by a company. One person volunteers to find a place and puts the word out about the meet up on Twitter. Everybody who hears about it, resends (or retweets) the announcement to their Twitter followers. It is word of mouth running on steroids. An average Tweetup will have 30-40 people, sometimes more, sometimes less.

Now let me tell you why I think it is a good idea for you to host Tweetups, or at least volunteer your restaurant for doing so. Don't worry, I am not going to ask you to give away free food or drinks. Most Tweetups are a one drink affair anyway. People are there to meet interesting and new folks and make new connections; they are not there to eat and drink into the night. Although a little bit of generosity on your part – maybe a couple pitchers of beers that will cost you less than \$50 – will not harm the general good karma flowing toward you.

But when you do it...who is coming to your restaurant? Who did you just place your restaurant in front of? The shining local stars of the word of mouth movement who appreciate the gesture. If nothing else, your restaurant name gets repeated hundreds of times locally on Twitter. Read the chapter on Twitter Marketing and especially the story of Kogi BBQ. Also, when people are at a Tweetup, they want their Twitter friends to join up...more people show up, and the more connections everybody makes, so guess what everybody is doing when they are at your restaurant? They are tweeting about the location – your restaurant – and asking everybody to join them.

Here are some tips to make hosting Tweetups a lot of fun and good business for you:

1. Find out who organized the last Tweetup in your city or metro area. Go to Twitter and search for your city name and the word Tweetup. Within 10 minutes you will see who the people were that encouraged everybody else to join them.

181

2. First *follow* these folks on Twitter so they know that you exist. And then direct message these folks using Twitter and volunteer your restaurant to host the next Tweetup.

3. Be upfront about your intentions. Tell them you feel it is a great opportunity for you to promote your restaurant and you also want to be involved in the local Twitter community as a way to learn more about online marketing.

4. When the Tweetup is going on – take pictures. Lots of them with everybody having a good time. Put them on your Facebook Page and of course on your Twitter account (use Twitpic.com).

5. Be generous. Ask your wine guys or your beer distributor to see if they can help you make the event an outstanding one and get a wine or beer tasting going on. I did a wine tasting to launch an online project and several months later people were still talking about it. It is not hard to make a party successful if you put your heart into it.

6. Don't ask anybody to plug your restaurant. It just makes people uncomfortable. Do the first five things right, play the gracious host, work hard making sure that everybody is having a good time, and you will end up with the buzz on Twitter in your local area.

Mommy Bloggers

Tom Peters, famous business author and management guru, has been saying for years that American business completely ignores women and baby boomers and focuses entirely on men as if they are the only ones with a wallet.

There are millions of women who blog about the life of a mother: working, raising kids, running a business, life / work / balance. The press had dubbed them all as Mommy Bloggers and although they are all different in their own rights, they represent a powerful group of online citizens to whom you should be paying close attention.

Just like the local scene on Twitter where people seem to know each other and want to finally meet face to face, local bloggers want to know each other also. It is closely knit community.

What I want you to do is take the lead here. Instead of waiting for a group of local mommy bloggers to come to your restaurant, why not approach them first and volunteer to organize a meet up for them once a month?

Think about this – you are putting your restaurant in front of people who are local, who spend a significant part of their day online, and who are active on Facebook and most likely Twitter. They probably have 125 to 700 Facebook friends who will hear about your restaurant indirectly. This is better than spending thousands on radio ads that may or may not hit. If you are promoting on your Facebook Page, knowing these groups of mommy bloggers in your local city will help you spread your promotions to lot of local folks very easily.

Here are some tips to make this happen:

1. Below are five popular mommy blog websites that you can use to find local mommy bloggers in your area:

    a. http://www.blogher.com/

    b. http://www.sheblogs.org/

c. http://www.themomblogs.com/

d. http://www.cafemom.com/

e. http://www.momblognetwork.com/

2. Build a list of mommy bloggers in your area.

3. Send them a short, polite email about your intention of hosting a local mommy blog meetup. Here is a template:

"Hi Jennifer:

My name is Doug Lyndon and I own a small French bistro in La Mesa in the San Diego County. I would love to volunteer my restaurant for hosting a local mommy blog meetup in the local San Diego area. I will also organize a small wine tasting for everybody that day. I am doing this for two reason: #1 I am very actively learning everything I can about online marketing and social media for marketing my restaurant so hanging out with a room full of online citizens like yourself would only help me and also it will bring lots of new people like yourself to my restaurant and hopefully you will like the experience enough to come back again and tell your friends about my restaurant too.

I am thinking some date in mid-May, Tuesday or Wednesday around 6pm to 8pm. If you like this idea – let me know and as I am contacting other mommy bloggers in the San Diego County, I will keep in touch with you as this event becomes reality.

Thank you

Doug

Zinc Bistro

www.Twitter.com/ZBristro"

4. Do not do this unless you have set up either a Facebook Page or a Twitter account. I would prefer that you had a lively Facebook Page with pictures, some video and regular updates before you did that because the first impulse would be to check you out immediately on Facebook and your first impressions will be lasting.

5. As you can see from my email template, I am upfront about why I am doing this. There is no reason to lie or beat around the bush about your reasons. You are doing it because it helps your restaurant by putting it in front of local bloggers. What is wrong with that? Everybody wins. The bloggers will have a great time and you took the initiative to set the whole thing up.

Remember to take pictures of the blogger meetup and put them on Facebook. Get names of those who attended and tag the names - watch the video on TheFullRestaurantBook.com/ActionPlan on Facebook so they can share the pictures also.

local Food Bloggers

Anthony Bourdain is a celebrity chef who has a hit TV show, No Reservations, on the Travel Chanel. Tony also wrote one of my all time favorite books – Kitchen Confidential – about his 30 years as a cook and chef working in New York kitchens. Recently, Tony did an episode of No Reservations called Obsession. It is worth buying on iTunes for a couple of bucks to understand what you don't know is happening in your local city right now when it comes to local food bloggers.

Gourmet magazine closed last year. Although a whole lot of people gasped in amazement when a blue chip name like *Gourmet* magazine just died without a fight, I was not surprised. The majority of the online world is no longer going to mainstream magazines to find out what they should be eating. They are going to Yelp, Urban Spoon, or websites like Yahoo Local to read reviews from their local neighbors on what they should be eating tonight.

Food bloggers are one of the most powerful, under the radar force in local food journalism to which most restaurant owners are not paying any attention. They are people like you and me who have genuine interest in food and what people eat and how it is cooked, and they are ruthlessly honest about their quest to find great food in their local cities – be it the best homemade red sauce for a pasta dish or the best fish taco in Dallas. They are on the hunt to find all the great eating places with blog readerships in the hundreds and sometimes even thousands, and I can make a bet that anybody reading a food blog is a dedicated restaurant-goer who likes to eat out a lot.

ACTION PLAN

1. Google to find and read the local food blogs before you approach them. Twitter is a great place to find food bloggers too, as most bloggers use Twitter. If a blogger only likes Asian food and that is all she is writing about, and you have a gastro pub...well, you get the idea. You should not be bothering her.

2. Compared to thousands of people on Twitter, millions on Facebook and even 50-250 mommy bloggers, you are looking at a small number of local food bloggers who are actively writing about local restaurants. If you can find 10 in your local metro area, you are doing pretty well.

3. You should invite them to come and eat at your restaurant and review it on their food blog. I am asking you to comp 10-15 meals. It is not going to kill you. It is the same as running a mass mail coupon campaign that most likely ends up in trash bins, but this will have considerably more impact.

4. What is your signature dish? The one dish that is loved above all by everybody? What food do you love in your restaurant? Serve them that food.

5. Sit with them and tell them about yourself. How you started in the business and most importantly, tell them the story of the dish that they are eating: where it came from, what you changed, why people like it and why you think this is better than everything else out that is being served.

6. How would you treat two people from Bon Appétit or from your local newspaper if they were at your restaurant right

now? To me, these local food bloggers have more power with their local audience than anything. They are all active on Facebook, Twitter, and have blog traffic that is coming there specifically to read their opinions about the local restaurants.

CHAPTER 17
Lessons From Food Network
by Mark Ijlal

This is a chapter that I almost did not write. I think it will be the chapter that most restaurant owners are going to skip over. They are going to think, "Yeah…right, online famous…food network…who does Mark think I am? I am no Bobby Flay or Rachael Ray. I own a little steak house in Oregon. I am not getting famous."

You are not entirely wrong. You are not Bobby Flay or Mario Batali, but you don't have to be. You could be famous, not to millions but to a couple thousand people in your local cities around your restaurant, and that will fill up your restaurant night after night.

This is not a chapter about being featured on Oprah or on the cover of People magazine as the sexiest chef alive, but hey, you never know…

I don't think Rachael Ray would have ever imagined her career when she was cooking demo foods in a supermarket aisle for passing shoppers.

"But I Am Not A Celebrity Chef."

First, a little thing about overnight success and fame. What you see and think about fame is really the end result of an endless campaign. That is like seeing two presidential candidates on Election Day and not realizing that they have been at it, non-stop, for the last two years and possibly a good ten years before that.

Second, there is a big difference in being a mainstream

189

celebrity chef or a big name celebrity restaurant like Wolfgang Puck's Spago in Beverly Hills. You could just be famous in upstate New York and do just fine.

The Last Thing You Want Is To Be Another Restaurant

Why in heaven's name do you want to be another restaurant? Being famous at least for a business is the best thing that could happen to you. Why be just an Italian restaurant when you could be THE HOT ITALIAN restaurant every night that people drive to from not just your city, but from miles around you?

Call ten of your significant other friends, the ones who are not in the industry, and ask them to name ten restaurants in your category which are not chain restaurants. If you can get them to name five, I will be shocked.

You Don't Need Luck

Ten years ago you needed great food, an incredibly strong chef, decades in business, and an enormous amount of luck to be featured in a national magazine. Your chances of being famous hinged on a famous person falling in love with you and talking about you. Almost the same odds you have today of going out and buying a lottery ticket and hitting the jackpot.

What you need more than anything is a committed schedule – whether it is 10 minutes or 20 minutes every single day to do one thing online to promote your restaurant with the intent of branding your restaurant different from your competition.

Here are the biggest lessons I have learned from Food Network and the practical ways to implement them in your restaurant:

190

1. A Celebrity Chef Is A Chef Who Is On Tv

Rachael Ray, the biggest Food Network star ever, bigger than Emeril and everybody else out there, has never cooked in a restaurant kitchen. So? It does not matter. If you want to brand yourself differently, if you want to place your restaurant above all your competitors in your area, then the fastest and easiest way is to put yourself, your restaurant, and your food on the new TV: YouTube.

Read the chapter on Online Video again. Here is how it works: your first ten videos are going to be terrible, especially when you are doing them yourself with a little camera hooked into a tripod. That is fine. You just need to make peace with that little fact. Did you ever see the show on TV, Before They Were Celebrities...where they show auditions of famous actors and how bad they all were when they started?

Your video #11 will be lot better than video #1. Your video #29 will be 100 times better than your video #11. This is about practice, not talent. People become good in front of the camera and talking to the camera when they do a lot of it. That is the secret. A lot of it, back to back.

Without hesitation and without care. Get the DVDs of The Next Food Network Start previous seasons and watch them from beginning to end. You will be shocked to see how lousy all contestants are and how good they become in front of the camera after some practice and coaching.

Put videos on Youtube, embed them on Facebook, let people know you. Involve everybody in your restaurant in this adventure: business partner, significant other, chef, wait staff, manager...use everybody in your videos to boost your own confidence. Above all, have some fun.

2. Bland Is Boring

Anthony Bourdain, former chef and host of No Reservations, the #1 food show on cable, smokes and swears on camera and is not shy to do shots of vodka between meals. He admits being wasted more than once and he is not shy about talking about his cocaine addiction days. I am not asking you to sit down and make a list of every stupid thing you have done in your youth and start talking about it, but what I am trying to teach you is bland is boring...people remember stories and interesting personalities and both of these things are self created. Tony is loved because people appreciate that even though he is on TV on a major channel with a hit show, he has never pretended to be somebody he is not. He is not that knowledgeable about wine and he freely admits it. Think about it...most people in the restaurant industry would be embarrassed to admit that.

Kurt Kobain once said that trying to be somebody else is the waste of the person you are. Don't pretend to be a cheap knockoff of Bobby Flay – be yourself. Tell stories about your restaurant, about yourself, how you started, why you like this dish and why you don't like something also. You are an interesting person. Most people work very hard at making sure that nobody ever finds that out about them. Don't make that mistake.

3. You Get 'Discovered' When You Show Up

If your dream is to be featured in a review by the biggest newspaper in your metro area or to get to do a local TV segment – well, they are not driving down the interstate looking for you. They

192

are online and they will find you WHEN you are doing the things online that will catch their attention. I am more likely to book you for a TV segment when I see a video of you on YouTube. I am more likely to interview you when I type in San Antonio Restaurant in Facebook and you are the first one with 3,000 fans that pulls up right on top. *You get discovered when you are in the game doing the things that are expected of players, not sitting on the sidelines.*

Rachael Ray was doing demos in a supermarket aisle. A local TV station saw her and liked her energy. She got a local TV station gig. Then somebody sent Al Roker her tape and she got on Good Morning America and the rest is history. But, and this is a big but, she was in front of people doing demos long before she was on Food Network. Those demos gave her the confidence that later helped her ascend at Food Network. Nobody is coming to discover you and find your great restaurant. It is up to you to make your restaurant known. You don't need money. A Flip cam costs $100. YouTube is free. And you don't need to hire somebody to write you a script. You know more about food than anybody else in the five miles around you. What good is this knowledge if it does not help you fill up your restaurant night after night?

4. The Big Guys Can Do A Lot But They Can't Do This

Most restaurant owners have a huge list of what they don't have when it comes to big chains in their areas. The big chains have more money to throw away to TV and radio advertising; they can make better looking and more expensive color coupons; they have better looking websites; and they probably have a staff of 15 people sitting doing nothing all day but online marketing.

Oh my....that does not sound that good for you, does it?

Well, have you ever worked for a big company? They are slow in execution. Everything they do has to pass thousands of memos, committee decisions, and everybody is committed to one thing: not doing anything risky at all.

You have an advantage here of being agile when they cannot. If you decide to shoot five videos, one every day, and start putting them on YouTube starting from today, all you need to do is go to your local Best Buy and buy a Flip cam and a tripod. That, and signing up for a free YouTube account, is all you need to start. It would take six months for a big competitor to do the same. Don't count what you don't have. Use what you have already.

5. Become Known To The Right People First

The roads to disappointment start with wrong goals. If you are expecting a review in *Oprah* magazine after doing three videos, all you are doing is planting the seeds of frustration within yourself. You will have more leverage in attracting the right kind of fame to your restaurant when you are mentioned in local food blogs, on Facebook, and on Twitter, than in half a page mentioned in your local newspaper that is basically thrown into the trash before the day is over. Yeah, sure, it makes you feel great that your efforts are being recognized and there is nothing wrong in framing the story and hanging it in a prominent place, but it is a one time hit and that is all. Local food bloggers have a much more targeted audience – people who like food and enjoy going out to restaurants.

6. Be Known For Something

I was watching No Reservations and Tony Bourdain was in San Sebastian, Spain and then in Brittany, France and in both of these episodes (buy them on iTunes and watch them, it is beautiful television) Tony ended up talking to people who were making something incredible – barbeque, apple cider, or chocolate, and they were famous for one thing and one thing only. People traveled from miles away just to taste that one thing.

If you go to a local restaurant and ask a waiter what is good there, what is the first common answer? EVERYTHING. I mean come on; there is no way that everything on a menu could be that good. You have one or two dishes that are very, very good; everybody loves them. One of the things that Food Network and Top Chef typically do is ask chefs to cook their signature dish. What is your signature dish for your restaurant? And if you don't have one – today is a good day to make one of your most beloved dishes into one.

Think of it this way, there are lot of steak houses in your zip code and cities around you. What if you were famous, not known, but famous, for your marinated filet mignon? People came just to eat that and nothing else. So you can say something in one of your videos... "I don't care if you have eaten steak ten times in the last six weeks in different restaurants, there is nothing out there like our filet mignon."

Song writers have hooks in pop songs. You want to pick a dish and make it your 'hook' for people to come to your restaurant. Frankly speaking, the new generation of young restaurant goers is much different than the generations that came before them. This is a generation that was raised on Food Network and now they are reading Yelp, Chowhound, and Urban Spoon where most reviewers typically rave about their favorite dish, which becomes the dish that most new people will order because they read the review. And if they like it, they will shout it out on Facebook and then the circle repeats from there.

Keep your 6-page menu but make one or two dishes the stars of your restaurant solar system and point all the light and glory at them.

CHAPTER 18
Being Found Showing Up High Locally On Google, Yahoo And Bing
by Jacqueline Shaffer

How would you like Google to show your local Italian restaurant 8,735 times in 30 days to folks who are trying to find an Italian restaurant in their neighborhood by typing in such words as restaurant, Italian restaurant, and their zip codes? How would your restaurant's bottom line look if you were able to get this kind of exposure for free and only by investing a couple of hours?

That is exactly what happened to Maisano's Italian Restaurant. Just by claiming their restaurant listing on Google Places, Yahoo Local, and Bing Local, they sent a signal to all three search engines that they were open for business. Within a matter of weeks, their search engine ranking on all three started to climb. Within 90 days, they were ranking higher than their bigger and better funded competition.

How did Maisano's pull this off? And how can you go from being invisible to being the place found all the time on local searches?

This chapter will help give you a basic understanding of local search marketing. Long shrouded in mystery and technical terms – local search marketing is the secret sauce that can help your restaurant jump right ahead of your competition on all the big search engines in a matter of weeks. This would lead to more customers lining up at your door every day.

Is it possible for all consumers who are looking for a classic American burger, like at your Pub & Grill, to be given YOUR phone number, address, directions, hours, and coupon every time they are looking on Google, Yahoo and Bing? You bet – all you have to do is put a little effort into your local search marketing.

Going forward local search marketing is the most critical aspect of an overall marketing strategy for any small business. You are a local company – your customers, your bread and butter, so to speak, only live within a several mile radius of your location. Your target market is very specific – so is local search marketing.

Local search helps consumers get in touch with exactly the service they are looking for that is closest to them. Local search marketing is the process of using targeted online marketing efforts to consumers who are local to your place of business. Online local search marketing uses keywords unique to your business and targeted to a specific geographical area – where your business is located – right down to the neighborhood zip code. As a business owner, the key is to be the one consumers find at the top of their search results.

WHERE ARE YOUR GUESTS TONIGHT?

In 2008, the internet surpassed every other form of media as the tool most used by consumers to search for information. It is now over 80%.

Research shows when a local search component is used, such as when people add a city or zip code to their search request, their intent to buy rises to nearly 100%. They aren't just looking for general information anymore – they already know what product or service they need and they're just looking for a local business to fill it. In other words, if a customer is searching for a "vegetarian restaurant in 48103," they have already made the decision to purchase.

Search engines like Google and Yahoo recognize this and provide a list of those local businesses that searchers requested right on the top of the first page of their search results. Right in front of your customer, that's exactly where you want your business to be! Google even uses the searcher's own IP address to determine the most relevant local information to present in the search results. It is solid local search marketing that will get you into that sweet spot.

5 Major Local Search Marketing Mistakes By Small Business Owners

- **They don't claim their business online** – often your business has a generic listing, but until you claim it, you are not getting any ranking or search benefits from it. It's easy and it's FREE! A no-brainer - Go claim it! Better yet, update it; add pictures, video, hours, specialty, coupon or your promotions.

- **They have a web site, online page or ad, and they never update it.** Search engines like Google love fresh content and they give preference to those who are participating and active online. The time spent nurturing your site and online presence will be rewarded with higher visibility, better search rankings, and in turn, more customers.

- **They have a boring online presence, whether on their website, or in their ads.** You not only need an interesting site, a place that attracts interest, but grabs attention. People are more likely to stay and check out your message if you include color rich photos of other people having fun, wonderful delicious food. Even better, include video of happy people enjoying food and good times at your business, saying good things about you.

* **They don't tell people anything about themselves.** People do business with people and places they resonate with. People like to be able to make a connection. Tell them about you, show them pictures of you and your staff, give them a story about you and the restaurant, how it came to be, why it's important to you.

* **They don't give a reason to contact them.** When people find you online, you need to connect with them and convert them, you need to tell them what you want them to do – and give them a good reason why! Make sure your phone number is highly visible and above the fold. Provide an incentive through a promotion, an event, a coupon or contest – again, make sure this is eye catching and shows above the fold.

7 Things You Need To Know To Put Local Search Marketing To Work For Your Restaurant

Here are the 7 most important tips to get your restaurant to start showing up high when local customers are looking for you in their zip codes:

1. Claim your listing with Google, Bing & Yahoo local search

One very simple way to increase your good favor with Google and other major search engines is to claim your business in Google Places, Yahoo Local, and Bing Local. Think of it as your own personal Yellow Pages listing that you can edit anytime. It's easy and free to update your listing and allows you to add your hours of operation, specialty information, coupons, and even pictures of happy customers dining at your business.

If you have tried typing your restaurant's name in Google and got a box full of restaurant listings and maps to their locations – that is all coming from Google Places. Claiming your listing at Google Places (www.Google.com/places) is the first step that can help you to start showing up on the Google map 7-pack listings at the top of most search result pages – a huge step toward eliminating your invisibility. Go to TheFullRestaurantBook.com/ActionPlan and watch the 3 short tutorial videos on how to setup Google Places, Yahoo Local, and Bing Local for your business. My company provides these services to local businesses in many industries (www.FindMeFamous) and our clients get fast results just by adding this first step to their online marketing plan. You go from being not found on Google to being one of the first pages within a matter of weeks.

2. Own a Search Engine Friendly Website

A dedicated business website is the anchor to your online presence. Developing a compelling website integrated with search engine optimization (SEO) will attract search traffic and bring the most qualified visitors to your site – those who are already motivated to buy. All other online marketing will be linked together to leverage one another, but will be ultimately tied to your anchor website. A well designed and optimized site will not only provide good search rankings, so visitors can find you easily, but will convert visitors into customers. A good, productive website need not be flashy or zillions of pages. A simple one or two page site with proper format and content can often do the job.

3. Be Found Everywhere in Local Directories

To develop a strong online presence, you can't be listed in just one or two places, but instead need to be found across the web. Be sure your business is accurately listed on other websites, review sites, and search directories specific to your specialty. Restaurants, for instance, should promote themselves at sites like Urban Spoon, BooRah, or Yelp as much as they would Google and Yahoo. These local search sites provide descriptions and reviews that help to form your online reputation, but are unique to your industry. Reviews will be read and used by people who have something to say about you and those that want to know what experiences others had with you – the good, bad, and ugly.

Keep in mind that customer reviews are seen as votes of confidence by search engines like Google. The more online "confidence" you acquire, the higher you're likely to rank in search results. A customer's experience with you provides credibility to those thinking about visiting you. Those reviews will help them make a decision to buy with you or not. Paying attention to these sites is vital to managing a positive online image and overall reputation.

4. Show up locally on mobile phones

This is ideally suited to the local restaurant owner. More and more consumers are using their mobile devices while they are out to make decisions about where they are going. A carload of foodies want to hit the best local Mexican restaurant in town; they are searching on their Blackberry and iPhones. Whoever shows up in the online search results nearby and with good reviews, and even better, with an incentive to come by (i.e., coupon), is going to get their business. Mobile devices are becoming more sophisticated all the time and are only expected to continue to grow in use and popularity.

5. Traffic reporting and Analytics

Google Places tells you exactly how many people were looking for you last month, how many of them asked for driving directions to your restaurant, which zip codes these searches were coming from, and it tells you all this for free. If you already have a website, ask your web designer or the company that sold you the website if they have installed Google Analytics on your restaurant website. To not have this free tool on your website is like having a restaurant with all the lights off.

These free tools are used to see and measure what's working with your online marketing, what's not working, and what can be done to convert more visitors into paying customers. Good reporting helps you keep track of what marketing dollars are bringing you the biggest bang for your buck.

6. Reputation management

Does it matter what folks say about you online? Of course, no one wants a bad review, but if it's warranted, don't underestimate the value of that input. Welcoming feedback provides an opportunity for your business to grow, to show your customers they matter, and to identify areas for improvement. Customer comments can help you to stay ahead of current trends as well as help you know what's working well. Taking an active role with your online reputation and responding accordingly provides you an edge over your competition that is not getting that kind of valuable insight.

7. Local Searches on Social Networks

Social networking is your online word of mouth, and small business can no longer ignore its importance in local search marketing. Many of the sites in your vertical local search, as well as Google and Yahoo, blur the line between social media and local search with the ability of users to review their experiences. Social networks like Facebook and Twitter are being used for recommendations and experience information shared quickly from one customer to another.

ACTION STEPS FOR PUTTING LOCAL SEARCH MARKETING TO WORK FOR YOU

1. Go to www.Google.com/places and create a free account.

2. Google will find your restaurant name, address and phone number and ask you to verify if all the information is correct.

3. Next add location, hours, parking information or anything else you feel will help your guests.

4. Add pictures. Lots of them.

5. If you have a video about your restaurant that is currently uploaded on YouTube – add the link here. Google owns YouTube and they make it really easy to do so. Just copy the link over.

6. When you click SAVE, Google will call your restaurant and give you a code. Punch in the code and your listing will become active within 48 hours. This verification process is done to ensure that none of your competition can poach off your listing.

7. Now that you have claimed your listing with Google, you can log in to your account and see all the valuable information: how many people are finding you locally, how many people are asking for driving directions, etc., for free in your Google Places account.

Google recently added some cool new features to their local search marketing. Go to our website to read all about them at TheFullRestaurantBook.com/ActionPlan

8. We also created 3 short videos to help you get these 7 steps done fast and also to help you set up Bing Local and Yahoo Local which are almost identical to Google Places. Find all three videos at TheFullRestaurantBook/ActionPlan

As a marketing specialist, Jacqueline Shaffer helps independent restaurant owners get more customers through targeted local search marketing integrated with online and offline marketing strategies.

With her 'Find Me Famous' services, she helps businesses cultivate a strong local presence – to become Famous - in their own cities, so they are found first and most often by customers looking for their specialty.

Being found at the top of online searches is just one component of a multi-faceted approach she uses with restaurant owners to reach maximum local exposure that gets more guests seated everyday.

When she's not helping business owners to get locally famous, she's a soccer mom, rollerblading fanatic and enjoys investing in real estate. She currently resides in SE Michigan with her husband, son and retriever, Casey.

RESOURCES

Michael Thibault has been in the trenches of the food service industry for over 30 years. As a restaurant owner owning 6 Restaurants each with different concepts, themes all while simultaneously owning $3,000,000+ a year Catering Company. His restaurants concepts ranged from Pizzerias to Upscale California Cuisine and Wine Bar. His unique combination of experience with what "works" and "what doesn't" from a restaurant owners point of view is invaluable. Mr. Thibault sold his restaurants and catering company in 2006 and started a Full Service "Done For You" marketing company that specializes in helping today's restaurant owners increase their sales. His company successfully helps hundreds of restaurant owners each month with their Newsletters, Social Media and Kid's Club programs. All with no work on the part of the restaurant owner. Simply put, Michael Thibault increases sales for restaurants owners in today's economy by getting measurable results with "Done For You Marketing Systems" that work.

You can reach Mr. Thibault at The Done For You Offices at 1-877-478-7862

****

Urvi Mehta is a passionate Social Media Evangelist who thrives on teaching and consulting business owners and organizations on how to effectively use Web 2.0, social media marketing tools and social networks like Facebook, Twitter and LinkedIn to create buzz, traffic and profits while increasing their branding online.

Urvi Mehta is a co-founder of PR Easy. PR Easy is the client focused full service internet marketing company which serves clients in US, Canada, UK and Australia. At PR Easy we provide Training, Consulting and various Done-4-You services which radically increases client's presence online which gets them massive exposure and web traffic to their website. PR Easy focuses on creating marketing campaigns which results into very qualified prospects for their clients thus increasing client's bottom line. PR Easy provides Search Engine Marketing, Search Engine Optimization, Social Media Marketing and Landing Page Creation services to business owners.

Discover How Restaurant owners are using Facebook fan page right now to bring more patrons to their business and create raving fans that come back over and over again.

Click on the link below to download A FREE Training Video On **"5 Key Elements Restaurant Owners Should Have On Their Facebook Fan Page"**

Visit http://www.PReasy.com/restaurantmarketing

You can reach Urvi and PR Easy at:

Phone: 734-743-1736
Fax: 734-322-0222

Email: urvi@preasy.com

Website: http://www.preasy.com
Blog: http://www.urvimehta.com

Facebook: http://www.facebook.com/socialmediagal
Twitter: http://www.twitter.com/urvimehta
LinkedIn: http://www.linkedin.com/in/urvimehta

****

As a marketing specialist, Jacqueline Shaffer helps independent restaurant owners get more customers through targeted local search marketing, integrated with online and offline marketing strategies.

With her 'Find Me Famous' services, she helps businesses cultivate a strong local presence – to become Famous - in their own cities, so they are found first and most often by customers looking for their specialty.

Being found at the top of online searches is just one component of a multi-faceted approach she uses with restaurant owners to reach maximum local exposure that gets more guests seated everyday.

When she's not helping business owners to get locally famous, she's a soccer mom, rollerblading fanatic and enjoys investing in real estate. She currently resides in SE Michigan with her husband, son and retriever, Casey.

You can reach Jacqueline Shaffer at phone: 734-786-9874.

Website: www.FindMeFamous.com/Restaurants
Email: Jaqui@FindMeFamous.com

****

For new updates, videos

and more resources,

Visit our book's website at

TheFullRestaurantBook.com/ActionPlan

Made in the USA
San Bernardino, CA
01 November 2015